Blueprints Visual Scripting for Unreal Engine

Build professional 3D games with Unreal Engine 4's
Visual Scripting system

Brenden Sewell

PUBLISHING

BIRMINGHAM - MUMBAI

Blueprints Visual Scripting for Unreal Engine

First published: July 2015

Production reference: 1210715

Published by Packt Publishing Ltd.
Livery Place
35 Livery Street
Birmingham B3 2PB, UK.

ISBN 978-1-78528-601-8

www.packtpub.com

Credits

Author
Brenden Sewell

Reviewers
Faris Ansari
Scott Hafner
Marcin Kamiński
Alankar Pradhan
Matt Sutherlin

Commissioning Editor
Neil Alexander

Acquisition Editor
Vivek Anantharaman

Content Development Editor
Divij Kotian

Technical Editor
Anushree Arun Tendulkar

Copy Editors
Hiral Bhat
Vikrant Phadke

Project Coordinator
Neha Bhatnagar

Proofreader
Safis Editing

Indexer
Rekha Nair

Production Coordinator
Aparna Bhagat

Cover Work
Aparna Bhagat

About the Author

Brenden Sewell is a lead game designer at E-Line Media, and has spent the last 5 years designing and creating games that are both fun to play and have educational or social impact. He has been building games since 2002, when *Neverwinter Nights* taught him an invaluable lesson about the expressive power of game design. In 2010, he graduated with a degree in cognitive science from Indiana University. Since then, he has focused on enhancing his own craft of game design while harnessing its power to do good in the world, and exposing more people to the joy the profession holds.

I would like to thank the following people for contributing to this book and making it a reality: Steve Swink (@steveswink), Jake Martin, Demetrius Comes, and Graeme Bayless for providing me the right mentorship to elevate me in my design practice; Logan Barnett (@logan_barnett) and David Koontz (@dkoontz) for pushing my knowledge of scripting to become a more versatile developer; the Packt Publishing staff and my technical reviewers for helping me to make this book a reality; the Unreal development community for being supportive and informative as we all endeavor to master this technology together; and my supremely supportive girlfriend Michelle, my parents who made this all possible, and all of my incredible friends for enriching my life.

About the Reviewers

Faris Ansari is an IT professional from Pakistan, who has skills and interest in Unity 3D, Unreal Engine, Cocos2d, the Allegro library, OpenGL, and other game development environments. He started his career as a game developer and worked on successful games that generated huge revenues. He also possesses the skills required for, and takes on new challenges while, working on new technologies, especially open source technologies.

Faris has reviewed the book *Learning NGUI for Unity*.

His hobbies consist of playing games, learning new things, and watching movies. He is very interested in working with fellow coworkers and friends on innovative ideas. His favorite saying is, "Every professional was once a beginner."

Feel free to contact him and discuss something innovative. He can be reached on LinkedIn at `https://www.linkedin.com/in/farisansari`.

> I would like to thank my friends and family for their continuous support and help.

Scott Hafner is a professional game designer with over 10 years of experience in the video game industry. Over the course of his career, he has worked as a producer, game designer, and level designer on a range of platforms and genres, including MMOs, third-person shooters, and RPGs.

> I would like to thank my fianceé for her continued encouragement and support in all that I do!

Marcin Kamiński is working for CTAdventure as a senior programmer and has his own company, Digital Hussars. Previously, he worked for Artifex Mundi, CI Game, and Vivid Games. His main fields of expertise are artificial intelligence and network programming. For 14 years, he has helped develop great games for PCs, consoles, and mobiles.

Marcin was also a reviewer of the books *Unity iOS Essentials* and *Unity 2D Game Development Cookbook*.

Alankar Pradhan hails from Mumbai, Maharashtra. He did his schooling from I.E.S.'s CPV High School. He is an ambitious person who loves interacting with new people, dancing, kickboxing, traveling, spending leisure time with friends, and playing games on PCs and mobiles. Games have always been a passion in his life. More than just playing games, how things worked was his main curiosity. Hence, he decided to pursue his career in this. Alankar completed his BSc honors in software development from Sheffield Hallam University, UK. He has done his master's in video game programming and management (video game director; BAC+5 equivalent) from DSK Supinfogame, where he undertook industry-oriented projects to increase his skill sets and gave his best to do so. Alankar worked as a game programming intern at Walt Disney, India. During his internship, he was working on a live project called *Hitout Heroes*. His name was added to the credits due to his noticeable work accomplished. He also interned as a game programmer with DSK Green Ice Games, and then went on to work as a video game programmer on a game targeted at PCs and consoles. This game, *Death God University (D.G.U)*, was released on July 1, 2015. Another project he is working on is *The Forsaken Mountains*.

Alankar has worked on many small projects in teams as well as individually to sharpen his own skills in various languages, such as C#, C++, Java, Unreal scripting, Python, Lua, Groovy/Grails, HTML5/CSS and so on. He is familiar with engines such as Unity3D, Unreal Development Kit, and Visual Studio and SDKs such as NetBeans, Eclipse, and Wintermute. In 2013, his dissertation work on *Comparison between Python and Lua in Gaming Industry* got published as a book. He has worked with Packt Publishing previously as a technical reviewer of *Creating E-Learning Games With Unity* and *Learning Unreal Engine iOS Game Development*.

Other than this, Alankar likes to read, listen to music, and write poems and short stories at times. He has his own website at http://alan.poetrycraze.com, where he posts his poems. He has also published a book, *The Art Of Lost Words*, which is available on Amazon.com.

His e-mail ID is alankar.pradhan@gmail.com. You can visit his portfolio site at alankarpradhan.wix.com/my-portfolio or contact him on Facebook at www.facebook.com/alankar.pradhan.

We are so often caught up in our aim that we forget to appreciate the journey, especially the people we meet on the way. Appreciation is a wonderful feeling, and it's way better if we don't overlook it. I hereby like to take this opportunity to acknowledge the people who directed me and inspired me in this initiative.

I would like to express my sincere thanks to my parents, who always instilled and believed in me. I am also thankful to my friends for their constant support and encouraging words that helped me reach this level.

Last but not least, I would like to thank all the people who are directly or indirectly involved in this book and helped me in some way or another.

Matt Sutherlin has been working in the games industry over the last decade, where he's served roles ranging from a QA and scripter to an engine programmer and a technical artist. Most recently, he has had a strong focus on graphics technology, working on engine renderers, art pipelines, and shaders for AAA titles such as *Heroes of the Storm* and *Halo 5: Guardians*.

I would like to thank my wife, Megan, and parents, Mike and Mary Lynn, for years of support, patience, and understanding; I wouldn't be where I am without you. I'd also like to thank Alan Wolfe for being an unending stream of cool programming tricks and insightful algorithms and for generally being a really great friend.

www.PacktPub.com

Support files, eBooks, discount offers, and more

For support files and downloads related to your book, please visit www.PacktPub.com.

Did you know that Packt offers eBook versions of every book published, with PDF and ePub files available? You can upgrade to the eBook version at www.PacktPub.com and as a print book customer, you are entitled to a discount on the eBook copy. Get in touch with us at service@packtpub.com for more details.

At www.PacktPub.com, you can also read a collection of free technical articles, sign up for a range of free newsletters and receive exclusive discounts and offers on Packt books and eBooks.

https://www2.packtpub.com/books/subscription/packtlib

Do you need instant solutions to your IT questions? PacktLib is Packt's online digital book library. Here, you can search, access, and read Packt's entire library of books.

Why subscribe?

- Fully searchable across every book published by Packt
- Copy and paste, print, and bookmark content
- On demand and accessible via a web browser

Free access for Packt account holders

If you have an account with Packt at www.PacktPub.com, you can use this to access PacktLib today and view 9 entirely free books. Simply use your login credentials for immediate access.

Table of Contents

Preface

Game engines, such as Unreal Engine 4 — as the tools that power the creation of the commercial games we love to play — are becoming increasingly accessible to both experienced and novice game developers outside of the traditional studio environment. Previous versions of Unreal Engine have powered many of the most popular console and PC games released over the last decade, and the newest version contains the tools for funneling this power into the hands of as many aspiring developers as possible. The most transformative of these tools is the Blueprints Visual Scripting system, which allows people who are not full-time programmers to create and implement the mechanics, interfaces, and interactions of a game.

Taking a step-by-step approach, this book will guide you through the process of using the visual nodes that make up Blueprint behavior, and link them together to create game mechanics, user interfaces, and more. In this process, you will be learning all the skills you need to get started with developing games in Unreal Engine 4 using Blueprints.

Starting with a basic first-person shooter template, each chapter will extend the prototype to create an increasingly complex and robust game experience. You will progress from creating basic shooting mechanics to gradually more complex systems that will generate user interface elements and intelligent enemy behavior. By focusing on universally applicable skills, the expertise you will develop in utilizing Blueprints can translate to other types of genres. By the time you finish this book, you will have a fully functional first-person shooter and the skills necessary to expand on the game to develop an entertaining, memorable experience for your players.

What this book covers

Chapter 1, Object Interaction with Blueprints, begins the book by covering how to bring new objects into a level to help build the world in which the game will be set. We move on to manipulating materials on objects, first through the object editor, and then by triggering during runtime via Blueprints.

Chapter 2, Enhancing Player Abilities, teaches you how to use Blueprints to generate new objects during gameplay, and link actions in Blueprints to player control inputs. You also learn to create Blueprints that allow objects to react to collisions with our generated projectiles.

Chapter 3, Creating Screen UI Elements, demonstrates setting up a Graphical User Interface (GUI) that will track the player's health, stamina, ammo, and current objective. Here, you learn how to set up a basic user interface using Unreal's GUI editor and how to use Blueprints to link the interface to the gameplay values.

Chapter 4, Creating Constraints and Gameplay Objectives, covers how to constrain the player's abilities, define the gameplay objectives for a level, and track those objectives via Blueprints that interact with the GUI elements created in the previous chapter. We walk through setting up collectible ammo packs that will refill the ammo of the player's gun, as well as utilizing the level Blueprint to define a win condition for our game.

Chapter 5, Making Moving Enemies with AI, is a crucial chapter that covers how to create an enemy zombie AI that will pursue the player around the level. We walk through setting up a navigation mesh on our level, and see how to use Blueprints to get enemies to traverse between patrol points.

Chapter 6, Upgrading the AI Enemies, shows how to create a compelling experience by modifying the zombie AI to have states in order to give the zombies a little more intelligence. In this chapter, we set up the patrol, searching, and attack states for the zombies using visual and auditory detection. Additionally, we explore how to make new enemies appear gradually, as the game is playing.

Chapter 7, Tracking Game States and Applying Finishing Touches, adds the finishing touches necessary to make our game a complete experience, before we finalize our game for release. In this chapter, we create rounds that will make the game increasingly difficult, game saves so that the player can save their progress and return, and player death to make the game's challenge meaningful.

Chapter 8, Building and Publishing, covers how to optimize graphics settings to get our game performing and looking at its best. Then, we explain how to create a sharable build of the game, and share some advice on how to continue progressing past the confines of this book on your way to becoming an accomplished game developer!

What you need for this book

This book is an Unreal Engine 4-focused title, which means you only need a copy of Unreal Engine to get started. Unreal Engine 4 can be downloaded for free from `https://www.unrealengine.com/`, and comes with everything you need to follow along with the book. This book was made using version 4.7.6 of Unreal Engine 4, and as such, it does not account for features added or removed in subsequent versions of the software.

Who this book is for

Whether you are brand new to game development or just unexposed to Unreal Engine 4's Blueprint Visual Scripting system, this is a great place to start learning how to build complex game mechanics quickly and easily without writing any text code. No programming experience required!

Conventions

In this book, you will find a number of text styles that distinguish between different kinds of information. Here are some examples of these styles and an explanation of their meaning.

Code words in text, database table names, folder names, filenames, file extensions, pathnames, dummy URLs, user input, and Twitter handles are shown as follows: "I named the project `BlueprintScripting` and stored it in the default `Unreal Projects` folder for OS X."

New terms and **important words** are shown in bold. Words that you see on the screen, for example, in menus or dialog boxes, appear in the text like this: " Now click on the **Library** tab, find the yellow **Install** button (as seen in the following screenshot), and click on it."

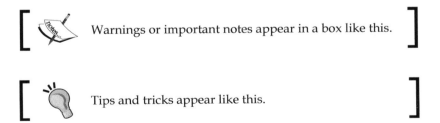

Warnings or important notes appear in a box like this.

Tips and tricks appear like this.

Reader feedback

Feedback from our readers is always welcome. Let us know what you think about this book—what you liked or disliked. Reader feedback is important for us as it helps us develop titles that you will really get the most out of.

To send us general feedback, simply e-mail feedback@packtpub.com, and mention the book's title in the subject of your message.

If there is a topic that you have expertise in and you are interested in either writing or contributing to a book, see our author guide at www.packtpub.com/authors.

Customer support

Now that you are the proud owner of a Packt book, we have a number of things to help you to get the most from your purchase.

Downloading the example code

You can download the example code files from your account at http://www.packtpub.com for all the Packt Publishing books you have purchased. If you purchased this book elsewhere, you can visit http://www.packtpub.com/support and register to have the files e-mailed directly to you.

Downloading the color images of this book

We also provide you with a PDF file that has color images of the screenshots/diagrams used in this book. The color images will help you better understand the changes in the output. You can download this file from http://www.packtpub.com/sites/default/files/downloads/6018OT_ColoredImages.pdf.

Errata

Although we have taken every care to ensure the accuracy of our content, mistakes do happen. If you find a mistake in one of our books—maybe a mistake in the text or the code—we would be grateful if you could report this to us. By doing so, you can save other readers from frustration and help us improve subsequent versions of this book. If you find any errata, please report them by visiting http://www.packtpub.com/submit-errata, selecting your book, clicking on the **Errata Submission Form** link, and entering the details of your errata. Once your errata are verified, your submission will be accepted and the errata will be uploaded to our website or added to any list of existing errata under the Errata section of that title.

To view the previously submitted errata, go to https://www.packtpub.com/books/content/support and enter the name of the book in the search field. The required information will appear under the **Errata** section.

Piracy

Piracy of copyrighted material on the Internet is an ongoing problem across all media. At Packt, we take the protection of our copyright and licenses very seriously. If you come across any illegal copies of our works in any form on the Internet, please provide us with the location address or website name immediately so that we can pursue a remedy.

Please contact us at copyright@packtpub.com with a link to the suspected pirated material.

We appreciate your help in protecting our authors and our ability to bring you valuable content.

Questions

If you have a problem with any aspect of this book, you can contact us at questions@packtpub.com, and we will do our best to address the problem.

1
Object Interaction with Blueprints

When setting out to develop a game, one of the first steps toward exploring your idea is to build a prototype. Fortunately, **Unreal Engine 4** and **Blueprints** make it easier than ever to quickly get the essential **gameplay** functionality working so that you can start testing your ideas sooner. To develop some familiarity with the Unreal editor and Blueprints, we will begin by prototyping simple gameplay mechanics using some default assets and a couple of Blueprints.

In this chapter, we will cover the following topics:

- Creating a new project and a level
- Placing objects in a level
- Changing an object's material through Blueprints
- Using the Blueprint editor and connecting Blueprints together
- Compiling, saving, and playing our game
- Moving objects in the world with Blueprints

Creating a project and the first level

Before we can begin setting up gameplay elements, we need to create a project that will contain the content of our game. To access Unreal Engine 4 and begin setting up our project, we must first open the Epic Games Launcher, which can be downloaded from the Unreal Engine 4 website (https://www.unrealengine.com/). From the Epic Games Launcher, click on the tab labeled **Unreal Engine**. If you are using Unreal Engine on your computer for the first time, you will see a grayed out-button labeled **Not Installed**. Along the left-hand side of the launcher, you will see options.

The **Library** tab is the location where you will be able to access the versions of the engine you have installed and the projects you have built. Now click on the **Library** tab, find the yellow **Install** button (as seen in the following screenshot), and click on it:

When the engine has finished installing, the **Install** buttons will change to **Launch** buttons, as shown in the following screenshot. Click on any of the **Launch** buttons to open the engine.

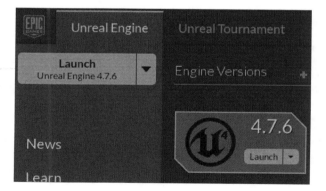

Setting a template for a new project

Once you click on **Launch**, you will be presented with the Unreal Project Browser. This will by default take you to the **Projects** tab, which will show you a thumbnail view of all the projects you have created, as well as any sample projects you might choose to install. For our purposes, we want to start a new project, so click on the tab labeled **New Project**.

From the **New Project** tab, you can select a template that will give you the initial assets to use for your game; or you can choose to start a blank project. You will see two subtabs under the **New Project** tab, labeled **Blueprint** and **C++**. Creating a project from the content within the **Blueprint** tab will start your project with a basic set of behavior built using Blueprints. The **C++** tab is used to create projects where at least some of the core types of behavior of the game are going to be built using the C++ programming language. Since we quickly want to get a prototype first-person shooter up and running without having to build the basic controls from scratch, we should ensure that we have the tab labeled **Blueprint** selected. Then we choose the **First Person** template, as shown here:

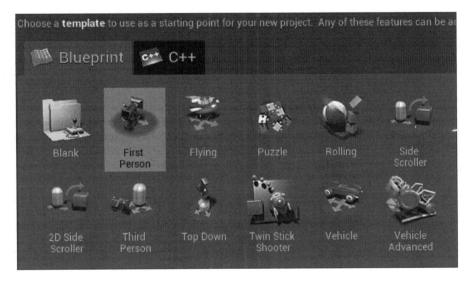

Making sense of the project settings

The next step is to adjust the project settings to our liking. The three gray boxes below the template selector allow us to select the class of hardware we are targeting (desktop/console or mobile/tablet), the graphics scalability, and whether we want to create our project with or without starter content. Leave these settings at their default values (**Desktop/Console**, **Maximum Quality**, and **With Starter Content**). Below these, you will see a folder path field used to designate where you would like to store your project on your hard drive, and a name field to input the name by which your project will be known. I named the project `BlueprintScripting` and stored it in the default `Unreal Projects` folder for OS X, as shown in this screenshot:

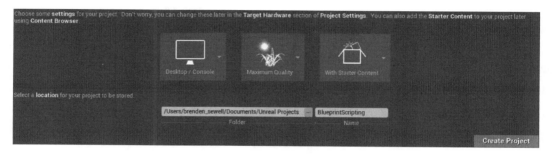

Creating the project

Now that we have a template selected and the project settings set up the way we like, we can create the project. To do so, click on the green **Create Project** button. After the engine is done with initializing the assets and setting up your project, **Unreal Editor** will open **Level Editor**, where you can create and view levels, place and modify objects, and test your game as you modify it.

Pressing the **Play** button, as shown in the following screenshot, along the top of the toolbar, will allow you to try the default gameplay that comes built into the **First Person** template. This includes player movement, shooting a simple projectile, and using projectiles to apply force to primitive box objects. In play mode, the **Play** button will be replaced with a **Pause** button and a **Stop** button. You can press the **Pause** button to temporarily halt the play session, which can be useful when you want to explore the properties of an interaction or actor that you just encountered during gameplay. Pressing the **Stop** button will end the play session and take you back to editing mode. Go ahead and try playing the game before we continue.

Adding objects to our level

Now we want to start adding our own objects to the level. The central panel you see in **Level Editor** is known as **3D Viewport**. A **viewport** allows you to see the 3D content of the game, and it is important that you become familiar with navigating inside this panel. The viewport can be navigated by moving the camera around using a combination of mouse buttons and its movement. Holding down the left mouse button and dragging the mouse pointer inside the viewport moves the camera view forward and backward, or left and right. Holding down the right mouse button and moving the mouse allows you to look around by rotating the camera. Finally, holding down either the middle mouse button or a combination of both the left and right mouse buttons will allow you to drag the camera up and down.

The simplest kind of object that can be dragged into the game world in Unreal Engine 4 is called an **actor**. An actor is a basic object with no inherent behavior other than the ability to be rotated, moved, and scaled, but it can be expanded to include more complex behavior by attaching components. Our goal will be to create a simple target actor that will change color when shot with the included gun and projectile. We can create a simple actor by going to the **Modes** panel. With the **Place** tab selected, click on **Basic** and then drag the object called **Cylinder** into the **3D Viewport**. This will create a new cylinder actor and place it in our level. You should see the actor in the **3D Viewport** as well as in the **Scene Outliner** panel, where it will be named Cylinder by default. Right-click on this object in the **Scene Outliner** panel, go to **Edit**, and then select **Rename**. Rename the Cylinder object to CylinderTarget, as shown here:

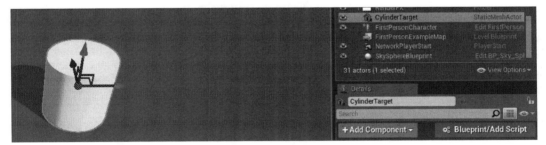

Exploring materials

Earlier, we set for ourselves the goal of changing the color of the cylinder when it is hit by a projectile. To do so, we will need to change the actor's material. A **material** is an asset that can be added to an actor's **mesh** (which defines the physical shape of the actor) to create its look. You can think of a material as paint applied on top of an actor's mesh or shape. Since an actor's material determines its color, one method of changing the color of an actor is to replace its material with a material of a different color. To do this, we will first be creating a material of our own. It will make an actor appear red.

Creating materials

We can start by creating a new folder inside the FirstPersonBP directory and calling it Materials. Navigate to the newly created folder and right-click inside empty space in the content browser, which will generate a new asset creation popup. From here, select **Material** to create a new material asset. You will be prompted to give the new material a name, which I have chosen to call TargetRed.

Material properties and Blueprint nodes

Double-click on **TargetRed** to open a new editor tab for editing the material, like this:

You are now looking at **Material Editor**, which shares many features and conventions with Blueprints. The center of this screen is called the **grid**, and this is where we will place all the objects that will define the logic of our Blueprints. The initial object you see in the center of the grid screen, labeled with the name of the material, is called a **node**. This node, as seen in the previous screenshot, has a series of **input pins** that other material nodes can attach to in order to define its properties.

To give the material a color, we will need to create a node that will give information about the color to the input labeled **Base Color** on this node. To do so, right-click on empty space near the node. A popup will appear, with a search box and a long list of expandable options. This shows all the available Blueprint node options that we can add to this Material Blueprint. The search box is context sensitive, so if you start typing the first few letters of a valid node name, you will see the list below shrink to include only those nodes that include those letters in the name. The node we are looking for is called `VectorParameter`, so we start typing this name in the search box and click on the **VectorParameter** result to add that node to our grid:

A vector parameter in the **Material Editor** allows us to define a color, which we can then attach to the **Base Color** input on the tall material definition node. We first need to give the node a color selection. Double-click on the black square in the middle of the node to open **Color Picker**. We want to give our target a bright red color when it is hit, so either drag the center point in the color wheel to the red section of the wheel, or fill in the RGB or Hex values manually. When you have selected the shade of red you want to use, click on **OK**. You will notice that the black box in your vector parameter node has now turned red.

> **Downloading the example code**
>
> You can download the example code fies from your account at http://www.packtpub.com for all the Packt Publishing books you have purchased. If you purchased this book elsewhere, you can visit http://www.packtpub.com/support and register to have the fies e-mailed directly to you.

To help ourselves remember what parameter or property of the material our vector parameter will be defining, we should name it color. You can do this by ensuring that you have the vector parameter node selected (indicated by a thin yellow highlight around the node), and then navigating to the **Details** panel in the editor. Enter a value for **Parameter Name**, and the node label will change automatically:

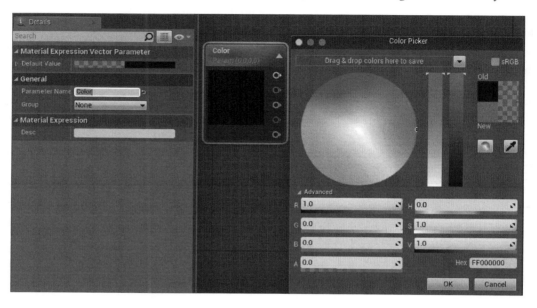

The final step is to link our color vector parameter node to the base material node. With Blueprints, you can connect two nodes by clicking and dragging one output pin to another node's input pin. Input pins are located on the left-hand side of a node, while output pins are always located to the right. The thin line that connects two nodes that have been connected in this way is called a **wire**. For our material, we need to click and drag a wire from the top output pin of the color node to the **Base Color** input pin of the material node, as shown in the following screenshot:

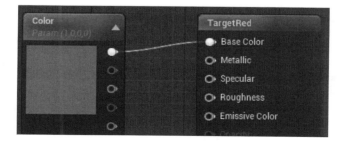

Adding substance to our material

We can optionally add some polish to our material by taking advantage of some of the other input pins on the material definition node. 3D objects look unrealistic with flat, single color materials applied, but we can add additional reflectiveness and depth by setting a value for the materials **Metallic** and **Roughness** inputs. To do so, right click in empty grid space and type `scalar` into the search box. The node we are looking for is called `ScalarParameter`.

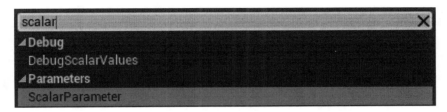

Once you have a scalar parameter node, select it, and go to the **Details** panel. A scalar parameter takes a single float value (a number with decimal values). Set **Default Value** to `0.1`, as we want any additive effects to our material to be subtle. We should also change **Parameter Name** to **Metallic**. Finally, we click and drag the output pin from our **Metallic** node to the **Metallic** input pin of the material definition node.

We want to make an additional connection to the **Roughness** parameter, so right-click on the **Metallic** node we just created and select **Duplicate**. This will generate a copy of that node, without the wire connection. Select this duplicate **Metallic** node and then change the **Parameter Name** field in the **Details** panel to **Roughness**. We will keep the same default value of **0.1** for this node. Now click and drag the output pin from the **Roughness** node to the **Roughness** input pin of the **Material** definition node.

The final result of our Material Blueprint should look like what is shown in the following screenshot:

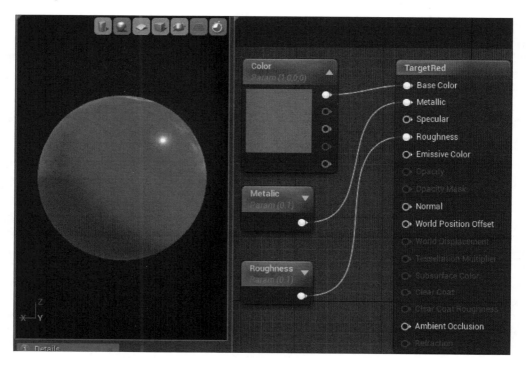

We have now made a shiny red material. It will ensure that our targets will stand out when they are hit. Click on the **Save** button in the top-left corner of the editor to save the asset, and click again on the tab labeled **FirstPersonExampleMap** to return to your level.

Creating our first Blueprint

We now have a cylinder in the world, and the material we would like to apply to the cylinder when shot. The final piece of the interaction will be the game logic that evaluates that the cylinder has been hit, and then changes the material on the cylinder to our new red material. In order to create this behavior and add it to our cylinder, we will have to create a Blueprint. There are multiple ways of creating a Blueprint, but to save a couple of steps, we can create the Blueprint and directly attach it to the cylinder we created in a single click. To do so, make sure you have the CylinderTarget object selected in the **Scene Outliner** panel, and click on the blue **Blueprint/Add Script** button at the top of the **Details** panel. You will then see a path select window.

For this project, we will be storing all our Blueprints in the Blueprints folder, inside the FirstPersonBP folder. Since this is the Blueprint for our CylinderTarget actor, leaving the name of the Blueprint as the default, CylinderTarget_Blueprint, is appropriate.

CylinderTarget_Blueprint should now appear in your content browser, inside the Blueprints folder. Double-click on this Blueprint to open a new editor tab for the Blueprint. We will now be looking at the Viewport view of our cylinder. From here, we can manipulate some of the default properties of our actor, or add more components, each of which can contain their own logic to make the actor more complex. We will explore components more in the next chapter; for now, we want to create a simple Blueprint attached to the actor directly. To do so, click on the tab labeled **Event Graph** above the **Viewport** window.

Exploring the Event Graph panel

The **Event Graph** panel should look very familiar, as it shares most of the same visual and functional elements as the **Material Editor** we used earlier. By default, the event graph opens with three unlinked event nodes that are currently unused. An **event** refers to some action in the game that acts as a trigger for a Blueprint to do something. Most of the Blueprints you will create follow this structure: Event (when) | Conditionals (if) | Actions (do). This can be worded as follows: *when something happens, check whether X, Y, and Z are true, and if so, do this sequence of actions.* A real-world example of this might be a Blueprint that determines whether or not I have fired a gun. The flow is like this: WHEN the trigger is pulled, IF there is ammo left in the gun, DO fire the gun.

The three event nodes that are present in our graph by default are three of the most commonly used event triggers. **Event Begin Play** triggers actions when the player first begins playing the game. **Event Actor Begin Overlap** triggers actions when another actor begins touching or overlapping the space containing the existing actor controlled by the Blueprint. **Event Tick** triggers attached actions every time a new frame of visual content is displayed on the screen during gameplay. The number of frames that are shown on the screen within a second will vary depending on the power of the computer running the game, and this will in turn affect how often **Event Tick** triggers the actions.

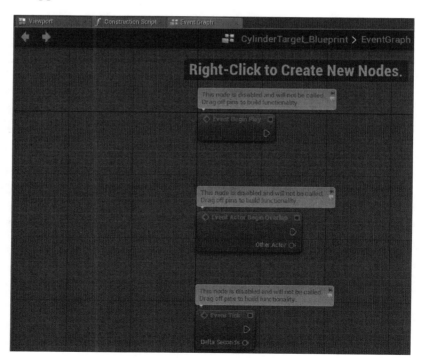

We want to trigger a "change material" action on our target every time a projectile hits it. While we could do this by utilizing the **Event Actor Begin Overlap** node to detect when a projectile object was overlapping with the cylinder mesh of our target, we will simplify things by detecting only when another actor has hit our target actor. Let's start with a clean slate, by clicking and dragging a selection box over all the default events and hitting the *Delete* key on the keyboard to delete them.

Detecting a hit

To create our hit detection event, right-click on empty graph space and type `hit` in the search box. The **Event Hit** node is what we are looking for, so select it when it appears in the search results. **Event Hit** triggers actions every time another actor hits the actor controlled by this Blueprint.

Once you have the **Event Hit** node on the graph, you will notice that **Event Hit** has a number of multicolored output pins originating from it. The first thing to notice is the white triangle pin that is in the top-right corner of the node. This is the **execution pin**, which determines the next action to be taken in a sequence. Linking the execution pins of different nodes together enables the basic functionality of all Blueprints. Now that we have the trigger, we need to find an action that will enable us to change the material of an actor. Click and drag a wire from the execution pin to empty space to the right of the node.

Dropping a wire into empty space like this will generate a search window, allowing you to create a node and attach it to the pin you are dragging from in a single operation. In the search window that appears, make sure that the **Context Sensitive** box is checked. This will limit the results in the search window to only those nodes that can actually be attached to the pin you dragged to generate the search window. With **Context Sensitive** checked, type `set material` in the search box. The node we want to select is called **Set Material (StaticMeshComponent)**.

> If you cannot find the node you are searching for in the context-sensitive search, try unchecking **Context Sensitive** to find it from the complete list of node options. Even if the node is not found in the context-sensitive search, there is still a possibility that the node can be used in conjunction with the node you are attempting to attach it to.

The actions in the **Event Hit** node can be set like this:

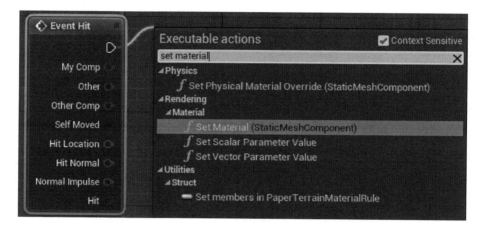

Swapping a material

Once you have placed the **Set Material** node, you will notice that it is already connected via its input execution pin to the **Event Hit** node's output execution pin. This Blueprint will now fire the **Set Material** action whenever the Blueprint's actor hits another actor. However, we haven't yet set up the material that will be called when the **Set Material** action is called. Without setting the material, the action will fire but not produce any observable effect on the cylinder target.

To set the material that will be called, click on the drop-down field labeled **Select Asset** underneath **Material** inside the **Set Material** node. In the asset finder window that appears, type red in the search box to find the **TargetRed** material we created earlier. Clicking on this asset will attach it to the **Material** field inside the **Set Material** node.

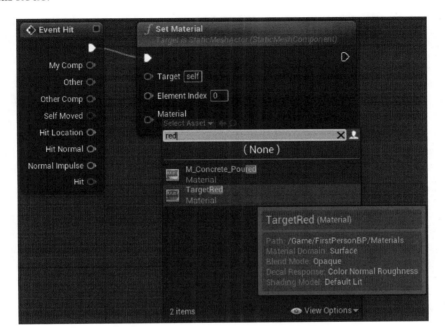

We have now done everything we need with this Blueprint to turn the target cylinder red, but before the Blueprint can be saved, it must be compiled. **Compiling** is the process used to convert the developer-friendly Blueprint language into machine instructions that tell the computer what operations to perform. This is a hands-off process, so we don't need to concern ourselves with it, except to ensure that we always compile our Blueprint scripts after we assemble them. To do so, hit the **Compile** button in the top-left corner of the editor toolbar, and then click on **Save**.

Now that we have set up a basic gameplay interaction, it is wise to test the game to ensure that everything is happening the way we expect. Click on the **Play** button, and a game window will appear directly above the Blueprint Editor. Try both shooting and running into the `CylinderTarget` actor you created.

Improving the Blueprint

When we run the game, we see that the cylinder target does change colors upon being hit by a projectile fired from the player's gun. This is the beginning of a framework of gameplay that can be used to get enemies to respond to the player's actions. However, you also might have noticed that the target cylinder changes color even when the player runs into it directly. Remember that we wanted the cylinder target to become red only when hit by a player projectile, and not because of any other object colliding with it. Unforeseen results like this are common whenever scripting is involved, and the best way to avoid them is to check your work by playing the game as you construct it as often as possible.

To fix our Blueprint so that the cylinder target changes color only in response to a player projectile, return to the **CylinderTarget_Blueprint** tab and look at the **Event Hit** node again.

The remaining output pins on the **Event Hit** node are variables that store data about the event that can be passed to other nodes. The color of the pins represents the kind of data variable it passes. Blue pins pass objects, such as actors, whereas red pins contain a Boolean (true or false) variable.

You will learn more about these pin types as we get into more complicated Blueprints; for now, we only need to concern ourselves with the blue output pin labeled **Other**, which contains the data about which other actor performed the hitting to fire this event. This will be useful in order for us to ensure that the cylinder target changes color only when hit by a projectile fired from the player, rather than changing color because of any other actors that might bump into it.

To ensure that we are only triggering in response to a player projectile hit, click and drag a wire from the **Other** output pin to empty space. In this search window, type `projectile`. You should see some results that look similar to the following screenshot. The node we are looking for is called **Cast To FirstPersonProjectile**:

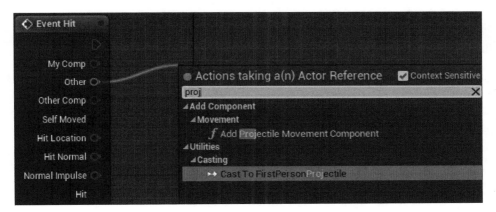

`FirstPersonProjectile` is a Blueprint included in Unreal Engine 4's `First Person` template that controls the behavior of the projectiles that are fired from your gun. This node uses casting to ensure that the action attached to the execution pin of this node occurs only if the actor hitting the cylinder target matches the object referenced by the casting node.

When the node appears, you should already see a blue wire between the **Other** output pin of the **Event Hit** node and the **Object** pin of the casting node. If not, you can generate it manually by clicking and dragging from one pin to the other. You should also remove the connections between the **Event Hit** and **Set Material** node execution pins so that the casting node can be linked between them. Removing a wire between two pins can be done by holding down the *Alt* key and clicking on a pin.

Once you have linked the three nodes, the event graph should look like what is shown in the following screenshot:

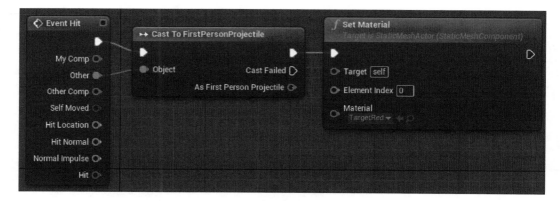

Now compile, save, and click on the play button again to test. This time, you should notice that the cylinder target retains its default color when you walk up and touch it, but does turn red when fired upon by your gun.

Adding movement

Now that we have a target that responds to the player shooting, we can add some sort of challenge to start making our project feel like a game. A simple way to do this is to add some movement to our target. To accomplish this, we will first have to declare that our target actor is an object that is intended to move, and then we need to set up logic within the Blueprint that will manage how it moves. Our goal will be to make the target cylinder move back and forth across our level.

Changing actor mobility and collision

To allow our target to move, we first have to change the actor's **Mobility** setting to **Moveable**. This allows an object to be manipulated while playing the game. From the main editor view, select `CylinderTarget_Blueprint`, and look at the **Details** panel. Underneath the **Transform** values, you can see a toggle for **Mobility**. Change this from **Static** to **Moveable**, as shown in the following screenshot:

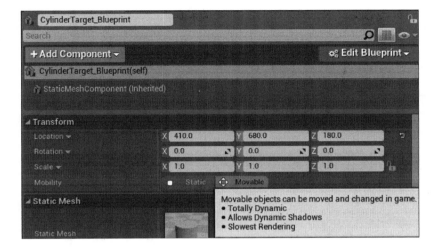

By default, basic actors that are placed in the world are set to **static**. "Static" means that the object cannot move or be manipulated during gameplay. Static objects are significantly less resource intensive to render, and this should be our default choice for non-interactive objects so that we can maximize frame rates.

It is important to note that the version of the target cylinder that we changed in the level is just one instance of the Blueprint template for the target cylinders that we have created. An instance refers to an actual object that has been created, whereas our Blueprints are descriptions of the kind of features that those instances will have once they are created.

Any changes we make to a target cylinder already inside the level will be made for that particular target cylinder only. To make changes to all future targets, we need to modify the Blueprint directly. To do so, open `CylinderTarget_Blueprint` again, either by navigating to the open tab in the editor, or by double-clicking on the `CylinderTarget_Blueprint` file in your `Blueprints` folder.

With the Blueprint open, we want to navigate to the **Viewport** tab located underneath the menu toolbar. Along the left side, you will see the **Components** panel, which lists all the components that make up this Blueprint. Since we want to edit a property of the physical object, or mesh, we click on component **StaticMeshComponent**. You will see a familiar-looking details panel. It includes the same properties and categories that we saw when we edited the target cylinder in the level editing interface. Here, we have to switch the same **Mobility** toggle, located beneath the **Transform** properties, from **Static** to **Movable**. This will ensure that all future targets created from this Blueprint will already be set to be moveable.

Because we want to target this object with our gun, we also need to ensure that the target is capable of being collided with so that our bullets don't pass through it. Still in the details panel, find the category called **Collision** and look for **Collision Presets** in the drop-down menu. There are many other options in this dropdown, and by choosing the **Custom** option, you can even set the object's collision interaction with different object types individually. For our purpose, we just need to ensure that this drop-down menu is set to **BlockAllDynamic**, which ensures that the mesh will register collisions with any other object that also has a collider.

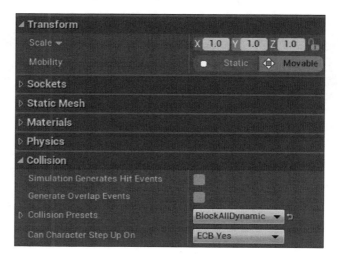

Breaking down our goal

Now that we have made our target moveable, we are ready to set up Blueprints that tell the cylinder how to move. In order to move an object, we will need three pieces of data:

- Where the cylinder currently is
- What direction it is supposed to move in
- How fast it is supposed to move in that direction

To understand where the object currently is, we need to get some information about the world itself. Specifically, what are the coordinates of the cylinder in the world? The speed and direction are the values we are going to provide to the Blueprint, though some calculations will be necessary to turn those values into information that is useful for the Blueprint to move the object.

Storing data with variables

The first step is to create the two variables we need: direction and speed. Find the panel labeled **My Blueprint**. You should see an empty category marker called **Variables**, with a + sign to the right. Click on that + sign to create your first variable.

In the **Details** panel, you will see a series of fields for editing your new variable. The four fields that we have to edit are the **Variable Name**, **Variable Type**, **Editable**, and **Default Value**. We want our first variable to contain information about the speed of movement, so name the variable Speed. For **Variable Type**, we want a variable that can hold a number that will represent our desired speed, so select **Float** from the drop-down menu.

Check the box next to **Editable** to enable the variable to be changed outside of this Blueprint. This will be useful for quickly adjusting the value to our liking once we start testing the moving target in the game. The **Default Value** category will likely not have a field, but will feature a message asking you to compile the Blueprint first. Do that, and a field for entering an initial value will appear. Change the default value to 200.0.

Using the same process, create a second variable called Direction. Choose **Vector** for **Variable Type**. A **vector** contains information about the X, Y, and Z coordinates, and in this case, we need to indicate the direction of change we want for the object movement. Make the direction variable editable and set **Default Value** to -10.0 for the Y axis.

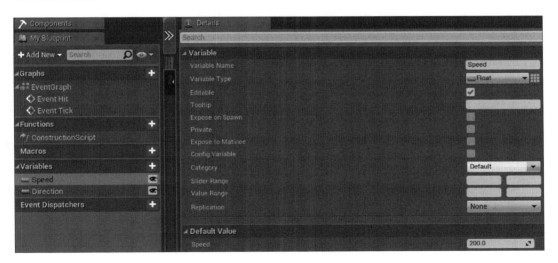

Readying direction for calculations

We will now explore the steps necessary to get the information we need to provide a movement instruction. It might look intimidating at first, but we will break down each section and see how each node fits into the larger goal.

The first calculation we need to perform is to take our vector value for direction and normalize it. **Normalizing** is a common procedure in vector math that ensures that the vector is converted to a length of one unit, which will make it compatible with the rest of our calculations. Fortunately, there is a Blueprint node that takes care of this for us.

Click on the **Direction** variable we created in the **My Blueprint** panel, and drag it into empty space in the event graph. A small popup will appear, prompting you to select **Get** or **Set**. We want to retrieve the value we set for the direction, so choose **Get** to create a node containing the direction variable's value. Click on the output pin of the **Direction** node, and drop it into empty graph space. Type `normalize` in the search field and select the **Normalize** node underneath the category labeled **Vector**. This will connect your `Direction` variable to a node that will automatically do the normalizing calculation for us.

It is good practice to leave comments on the sets of Blueprints as you create them. Comments can help describe what a particular set of Blueprints is intended to accomplish, which can be helpful if you are returning to a Blueprint after some time and need to make sense of your prior work. To leave a comment on a Blueprint, click and drag a selection box around the nodes you want to create a comment around to select them. Then, right-click on one of the selected nodes and select the bottom option, **Create Comment from Selection**.

Getting relative speed using delta time

To make our speed value relate to direction, we first need to multiply it by **delta time**. Delta time is based on the fact that the time taken between the frames of the gameplay can differ. By multiplying our speed value to delta seconds, we can ensure that the speed at which our object moves is the same, regardless of the game's frame rate.

To do this, drag the **Speed** variable onto the event graph and choose **Get** to create the speed node. Now, right-click on empty graph space and search for delta. Select the **Get World Delta Seconds** option to place the corresponding node. Finally, drag the output pin from either the delta seconds node or the speed node, and drop it into empty space. Type an asterisk in the search field (*Shift + 8* on most computers) and select the **Float * Float** node. Finally, drag the other output pin onto the remaining input pin of the new multiplication node to multiply these two values, like this:

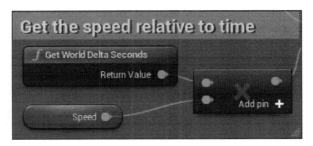

Translating the existing location

Now that we have a normalized vector direction and a speed value relative to time, we need to multiply these two values and then add them to the current location. First, find the **StaticMeshComponent** component from the **Components** panel and drag it onto the event graph. This will create a node from which we can extract any data contained within the mesh component of the object.

Next, we want to get the mesh's location. One of several ways to handle this is to look at the transform properties of an object and extract the location from there. Click and drag the blue output pin into empty space, and then type Get World. Select the **Get World Transform** option to create the node. A **transform** contains information about the rotation and scale of an object, in addition to its location. This will be useful because we want to ensure that we preserve the rotation and scale of our target even as it is moving, and we will need that data to create a transform value from our new movement information.

Now we want to break down the transform into its component parts so that we can use just the location in our calculations, while preserving the rotation and scale. Drag the output pin from the world transform node, and search for the **Break Transform** node to add to our graph.

Now we need to add the necessary nodes to add speed and direction to the location information we just extracted. Right-click on empty grid space and search and select the **Make Transform** node. This will mark the end of your calculations, so make sure that it is positioned to the right of all of your other nodes. The **Make Transform** node has three inputs, **Location**, **Rotation**, and **Scale**. The **Rotation** and **Scale** inputs should be connected to the rotation and scale output pins on the **Break Transform** node we created earlier.

Next, we need to multiply the Direction vector and the Speed float we calculated. Drag the output node of the **Normalize** node into empty space, and search using an asterisk. Select **Vector * Float** and connect the green input pin to the output of the float multiplication node that we used with speed.

Our final calculation step is to add Speed and Direction to the current location we calculated. Click on the yellow vector output pin of the new multiplication node, and drag it onto empty space. Search using + and select the **Vector + Vector** node. Ensure that one input pin of this addition node is connected to the previously mentioned vector multiplication node, and then connect the other input pin is connected to the **Location** output pin of the **Break Transform** node. Finally, drag the output pin of our addition node onto the **Location** input pin of the **Make Transform** node. When you are finished, the result should look like what is shown in the following screenshot:

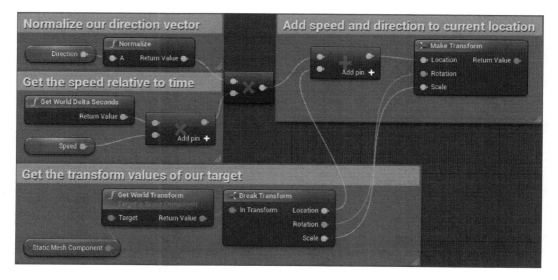

Updating location

Now that we have the transform calculated, we can adjust the location of our target actor by this value. We used delta time to make our speed and direction changes consistent across frames, and as a consequence, we can simply use the **Event Tick** node to fire our move action every frame. Right-click on empty grid space, search for `Event Tick`, and place the node somewhere to the right of your **Make Transform** node.

To move the actor, we will be using the **Set Actor Transform** node. Drag a wire from the execution pin of **Event Tick** to empty grid space, and search for `Set Actor Transform`. Place the node, and then connect the **Return Value** output pin on your **Make Transform** node to the **New Transform** input pin on the **Set Actor Transform** node, as shown here:

Changing direction

If you were to compile the Blueprint, save, and play the game now, what would you expect to see? The target cylinder would move according to our speed and direction as soon as the game began. However, since we don't have any instructions that cause the target to stop moving, it would proceed in the same direction for as long as the game runs, even moving through objects and out of the level we created! To address this, we need logic that will change the target's direction periodically. This will result in a target that moves back and forth between two points regularly, much like a shooting gallery target.

To do this, we have to set up two nodes that will set the direction variable we created to two different values. Drag the direction variable into empty grid space and choose the **Set** option. This will result in a node with *X*, *Y*, and *Z* axis fields. We can use them to change the value of the direction variable to be different from the initial default value that we gave it. We want two of these nodes, so drag the direction variable again into empty space, and then change the *Y* axis values of the two nodes to 10.0 and -10.0 respectively.

Now we need a way to switch between these two nodes so that the direction repeatedly shifts. The **FlipFlop** node was created for scenarios where we know we want to alternate between two sets of actions that execute exactly once before switching each time. This fits our use case here, so right-click on empty grid space and search for FlipFlop. Select and place the node. Then connect the **A** execution pin to one of the direction set node input pins, and the **B** execution pin to the other.

Finally, we need to ensure that there is some kind of delay between executing the direction shifts. Otherwise, the direction will change for every frame and the object will go nowhere. To do so, drag the input execution pin of the **FlipFlop** node into empty space and search for the **Delay** node. This node allows us to set a delay duration, in seconds, that will postpone the following execution commands by that length of time. Place this node before the **FlipFlop** node and give it a duration of 6 seconds. Placing this **Delay** node between our **Set Actor Transform** node and our **FlipFlop** node will ensure that the direction switch enabled by **FlipFlop** will occur only every 6 seconds. The final product should look like what is shown in the following screenshot. Once you are done, remember to compile and save the Blueprint.

Testing moving targets

Now that we have our Blueprint updated, we can test to ensure that the CylinderTarget object moves as expected. First, we will have to place the CylinderTarget object in a position that will allow it to move along the *Y* axis without bumping into other objects. The coordinates I used were 410 on the *X* axis, 680 on the *Y* axis, and 180 on the *Z* axis.

Note that these values will only work relative to the default layout of the First Person template map. If you have made adjustments to your own level, then you can adjust either the speed or the placement of the target in your level, and test until you find a good patrol spot. Click on Play. If the Blueprint is functioning correctly, you will see the cylinder move back and forth between two points at a steady rate.

One of the advantages of using Blueprints is that they create a template of functionality that can be used across multiple objects in a scene. Find CylinderTarget_Blueprint in the Blueprints folder and drag it directly onto **3D Viewport**. You will see another cylinder created, which inherits all of the functionality of our original cylinder target. In this way, we can rapidly set up multiple moving targets using the single set of Blueprint logic we created.

Summary

You have built your first prototype using Unreal 4 Blueprints. Congratulations! The amount of progress you have already made is commendable.

In this chapter, you created a project and an initial level using a first-person shooter template. You then set up a target object that reacts to the player's gunfire by changing appearance. Finally, you set up a Blueprint that will allow you to rapidly create moving targets. The skills you have learned here will serve as a strong foundation for building more complex interactive behavior in later chapters, or even entire games of your own making.

You may wish to spend some additional time modifying your prototype to include a more appealing layout, or feature faster moving targets. As we continue building our game experience, remember that you always have the opportunity to linger on a section and experiment with your own functionality or customizations. One of the greatest benefits of Blueprint's visual scripting is the speed at which you can test new ideas, and each additional skill that you learn will unlock exponentially more possibilities for game experiences that you can explore and prototype.

In the next chapter, we will be looking more closely at the player controller that came with the First Person template. We will extend the existing Blueprint that governs player movement and shooting with a gun that is tweaked to our liking, and produces a more interesting visual impact and sound effects.

2
Enhancing Player Abilities

In this chapter, we will expand upon the core shooting interaction that we created in the previous chapter by making modifications to the player character Blueprint. The player character Blueprint that comes with the `First Person Shooter` template initially looks complex, especially when compared to the relatively simple cylinder target Blueprint that we have already created from scratch. We will be looking into this Blueprint and breaking it down to see how each of its sections contributes to the player's experience and allows them to control their character and shoot a gun.

It would be quick and easy to just use an existing asset that works, without spending time understanding how it is accomplishing its functionality. However, we want to ensure that we can repair problems as they arise, and extend the functionality of the player controls to fit our needs better. For this reason, it is always advisable to take some time to investigate and understand any external asset you might bring into a project that you are building.

By the end of this chapter, we want to succeed in modifying the player controller, so that we can add the ability to sprint and destroy the objects we shoot with enjoyable explosions and sound effects. Along the way to achieving these goals, we will be covering the following topics:

- Player inputs and controls
- Field of view
- Timelines and branching logic
- Adding sounds and particle effects to an object interaction

Adding the running functionality by extending a Blueprint

We'll begin our exploration of the `FirstPersonCharacter` Blueprint by adding simple functionality that will give our players more tactical options for moving around in the level. At the moment, the player is limited to moving at a single speed. We can adjust this using Blueprint nodes that listen for key presses, and adjusting the movement speed attached to the `CharacterMovement` component of the Blueprint.

Breaking down the Blueprint character movement

Let's begin by opening the `FirstPersonCharacter` Blueprint, located in the same `Blueprints` folder as `CylinderTarget_Blueprint` from the last chapter. Find **FirstPersonCharacter** in the content browser, and double-click on the Blueprint. You will open **Event Graph** and see a large series of Blueprint nodes. The first group of nodes we will look at is bounded by the event graph comment labeled **Stick input**, as shown here:

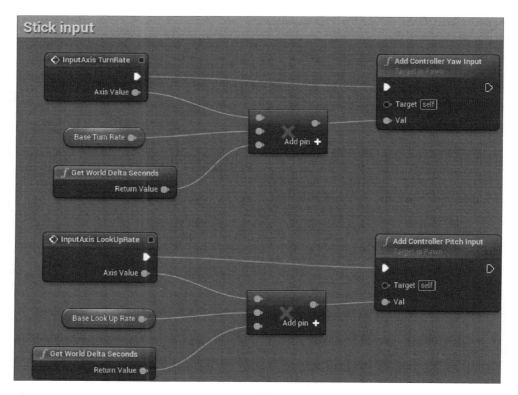

The red trigger nodes are triggered at every frame, and pass the values of **TurnRate** and **LookUpRate** from a controller input. These values are most commonly mapped to the left/right and up/down axis of an analog stick. Note that there are only two axis triggers. Detecting a look down or a turn left event is covered by these very nodes, and is represented as a negative number in the **Axis Value** that is passed.

Then, the values from the two axis triggers are each multiplied by a variable, representing the base rate at which the player is intended to be able to turn around or look up or down. The values are also multiplied by the world delta seconds to normalize against varying frame rates, in spite of the triggers being called every frame. The value resulting from multiplying all the three inputs is then passed to the **Add Controller Pitch Input** and **Add Controller Yaw Input** functions. These are the functions that add translation between the controller input and the effect on the player camera.

Below the **Stick Input** group of Blueprint nodes, there is another comment block, called **Mouse Input**, and it looks quite similar. **Mouse Input** converts input from mouse movements, as opposed to controller axis sticks, into data and then passes those values directly to the corresponding camera yaw and pitch input functions, without needing the same kind of calculations that were necessary for analog input.

Now let's look at the group of nodes managing player movement, as shown in this screenshot:

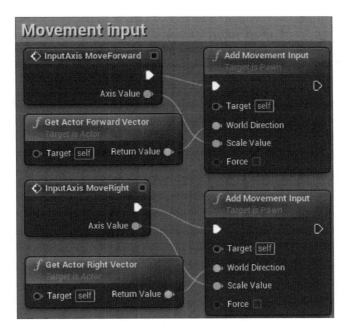

Functionally, these nodes are set up similarly to the stick and mouse input groups. The axis value is taken from the forward and right movement axis inputs on a controller or keyboard. Again, these nodes represent backward and left movements as well, in the form of negative values for the **Axis Value** outputs. The significant difference in movement translation is that we require the direction of the actor being moved, so that the degree of movement can be applied in the correct direction. The direction is pulled from the **Get Actor Vector** nodes (both forward and right) and attached to the **World Direction** input of the **Add Movement Input** nodes.

The last movement-related group of nodes to look at is the node group contained within the comment block labeled **Jump**. This group is simply made up of a trigger node that detects the pressing and releasing of the key mapped to jumping, and applies the `junction` function from when the button is pressed until it is released.

Customizing control inputs

We have seen how the `First Person` template has mapped certain player input actions, such as moving forward or jumping, to Blueprints to produce the behavior for the actions. In order to create new kinds of behavior, we will have to map new physical control inputs to additional player actions. To change the input settings for your game, click on the **Edit** button in the **Unreal Editor** menu, and select the **Project Settings** option. On the left side of the window that appears, look for the **Engine** category and select the **Input** option.

Inside the **Engine** category, in the **Input Settings** menu, you will see two sections under the **Bindings** category called **Action Mappings** and **Axis Mappings**. **Action Mappings** is for key press and mouse click events that trigger player actions. **Axis Mappings** is meant for mapping player movements and events that have a range, such as the *W* key and *S* key both affecting the **Move Forward** action, but on different ends of the range. Both our `Sprint` and `Zoom` functions are simple actions that are either active or inactive, so we will be adding them as **Action Mappings**.

Click on the **+** sign next to **Action Mappings** twice to add two new action mappings. Name the first one **Sprint**, and select the **Left Shift** key from the drop-down menu to map that key to your **Sprint** event. Call the second action **Zoom**, and map it to **Right Mouse Button**. Your **Action Mapping** inputs should match what is shown in the following screenshot:

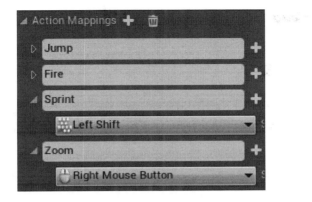

Adding a sprint ability

Now that we have a basic understanding of how the movement input nodes take the controller input and apply it to our in-game character, we'll extend that functionality with a player sprint. We'll be setting up a new series of nodes within FirstPersonCharacter Blueprint. They will look like what is shown in this screenshot:

First, we will need to create the trigger that will activate our sprint. Recall that we previously mapped the action sprint to the **Left Shift** key. To access that input trigger, right-click on empty grid space to the left of the other movement functions, and search for Sprint. Select the **InputAction Sprint** event to place the node.

Now we want to modify the movement speed of the player. If you try adding a new node and searching for `speed` with context-sensitive search turned on, you will find only those nodes that are meant for retrieving the maximum speed and checking whether it is being exceeded. Neither of these will help you set the maximum speed of the player. To accomplish this, we need to retrieve a value from the character movement component attached to the `FirstPersonCharacter` actor. Look at the **Components** panel of the editor and select **CharacterMovement (Inherited)**. The **Details** panel should change to look like a long series of variables, as seen in the following screenshot:

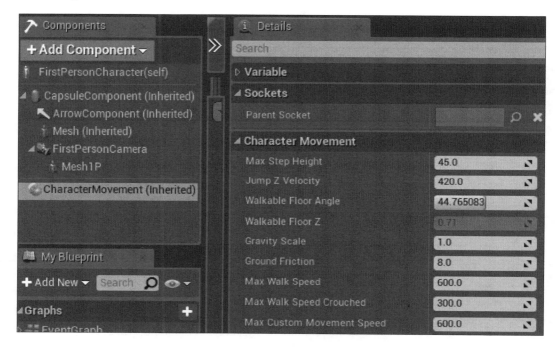

The (Inherited) tag at the end of the component name tells us that the functionality of this component was defined within a C++ script, rather than a Blueprint. This is common with many components that do the heavy lifting, with physics calculations related to movement or mesh definitions. If you are ever interested in seeing the code that drives an inherited component, you can select the **Open (filename).h** option from the right-click menu of the component.

In this list of variables, you can find **Max Walk Speed** close to the top. This is the value that determines that maximum speed at which the player can move, and it should be the target of our `Sprint` function. However, changing the value in the **Details** panel from the default of `600` would modify the player's movement speed consistently, regardless of whether left *Shift* was being pressed or not. Instead, we want to pull this value out of the character movement component and into our Blueprint's event graph. To do so, click on the component in the **Components** panel and drag it onto the event graph, near our **Left Shift** trigger. This will produce a **Character Movement** node, as seen in this screenshot:

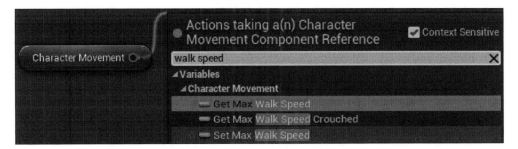

Click and drag the output pin from the **Character Movement** node to empty space, ensure that you have **Context Sensitive** checked, and type `walk speed`. This time, the **Set Max Walk Speed** action will appear. Select it to connect the **Character Movement** node to the new node setting the maximum walk speed value. Connect the **Pressed** output execution pin from the **InputAction Sprint** trigger to the input execution pin of the **Set Max Walk Speed** node to enable pressing left *Shift* to modify the maximum movement speed. Finally, change the **Max Walk Speed** value within the node from `0.0` to `2200` to provide a nice boost of speed over the default of `600`.

We also need to ensure that the player slows down again once the *Shift* key is released. To do so, drag the output pin from the **Character Movement** node again, and then search for and place another **Set Max Walk Speed** node. This time, connect the **Released** output execution pin of the **InputAction Sprint** node to the input execution pin of the new node. Then change the **Max Walk Speed** value from `0.0` to the default of `600`. To keep up with our good commenting practice, click and make a selection box around all four of our nodes, right-click, and select **Create Comment from Selection** to label the group of nodes `Sprint`.

Now compile, save, and press **Play** to test your work. You should notice a significant boost in speed as long as you press down the left *Shift* key.

Animating a zoom view

A core element of modern First-Person Shooters is a variable **FOV** (also known as **field of view**) in the form of a player's ability to look down the scope of a gun to get a closer view of a target. This is a significant contributor to the feeling of accuracy and control that modern shooters provide. Let's add a simple form of this functionality to our prototype.

In an empty section of grid next to your mouse input nodes, right-click, search for an **InputAction Zoom** trigger node, and add it. We want to modify the FOV value that is contained within the **FirstPersonCamera** component, so we go to the **Components** panel and drag **FirstPersonCamera** out onto the event graph.

Drag the output pin into empty space, search for the **Set Field Of View** node, and place it. Lowering the field of view gives the effect of zooming into a narrower area in the center of the screen. Since the default field of view value is set to 90, for our zoom, let's set the field of view in the set node to 45, like this:

Click and drag the output execution pin from the right-click trigger node to the input execution pin of the set node. Compile, save, and click on **Play**. You will notice that when you right-click, the FOV will snap to a narrow, zoomed-in view. Any instance where the main camera snaps from one position to another can be jarring for a player, so we will have to modify this behavior further.

Using a timeline to smooth transitions

To change the FOV smoothly, we will need to create an animation that shows a gradual change in the actor over time. To do so, return to the event graph of the **FirstPersonCharacter** Blueprint.

Press *Alt* and click on the **Pressed** output execution pin of the **InputAction Zoom** node to break the connection. Drag a new wire out from **Pressed** to empty space. Search for and select **Add Timeline** to add a timeline node. A **timeline** will allow us to change a value (such as the field of view on a camera) over a designated amount of time.

There are two primary ways of accomplishing animations in Unreal Engine 4. Timelines are perfect for simple value changes, such as the rotation of a door. For more complex, character-based, or cinematic animations, you would want to look into **Matinee**, the engine's built-in animation system. Matinee and complex animations are out of the scope of this book, but there are many dedicated learning resources available for using Matinee. I recommend starting with the Unreal wiki repository of related tutorials, available at `https://wiki.unrealengine.com/Category:Matinee`.

To change the value within the timeline, double-click on the timeline node. This will open up the **Timeline** editor. You will see four buttons in the top-left corner of the editor. Each of these will add a different kind of value to be changed over the course of the timeline. Because FOV is represented by a numerical value, we will want to click on the button with the **f** label (**Add Float Track**). Doing so will add a timeline and prompt you to label the value to be changed. Let's label this **Field of View**. We will now have to edit the values over different time intervals, as shown here:

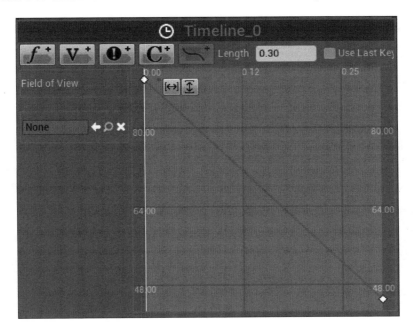

To accomplish this, hold down *Shift* and click close to the **0,0** point on the graph. You will see the **Time** and **Value** fields appear in the top-left part of the graph. This allows precision tuning of our timeline. Ensure that the time is set to exactly `0.0` and set the value to `90`, our default FOV.

We want the zoom animation to be quick, so at the top of the **Timeline** editor, find the field next to **Length** and change to value to 0.3 to limit the range of the animation to 0.3 seconds. Now press *Shift* and click at the end of the white area of the graph. Fine-tune the fields to 0.3 for **Time** and 45 for **Value**. Note that whole numbers entered in the **Value** field will automatically be translated into floating-point values that are nearly identical, as seen in the following screenshot. The difference is not large enough to produce any observable effect, so we don't have to concern ourselves with this translation:

Notice how the red line reflecting the value gradually slopes down from 90 degrees to 45 degrees. This means that when this animation is called, the player's FOV will smoothly transition from being zoomed out to zoomed in, rather than a jarring switch between the two values. This is the advantage of using timelines over changing the values directly with a set value Blueprint.

Now return to the event graph. We will want to connect our timeline into our set FOV operation, just like what is shown in this screenshot:

Drag the new **Field of View** output pin into the **Field of View** field in the **Set** node, overriding your value of 45. Now link the **Update** output execution pin from the timeline to the set node. This sets up the functions such that every time the FOV value is updated, it passes the new value to the set function. Because of our timeline setup, many values between 90 and 45 will be passed to set, enabling a gradual transition between the two extremes over 0.3 seconds.

Finally, we want the zooming to end when the right mouse button is released. To do this, drag the **Released** pin from the **InputAction Zoom** node to the **Reverse** pin of the **Timeline** node. This will cause the timeline animation to play in reverse order when the button is released, ensuring that we have a smooth transition back to our normal camera view. Also, remember to apply a comment to the node group, so that you remember what this functionality does if you revisit it later.

Now compile, save, and play to test the transition in and out of your zoom view by holding down the right mouse button.

Increasing the projectile's speed

Now that we have given the player character a new gameplay option to navigate the world, our focus will be back to the shooting mechanics. Right now, the shots fired from the gun on the controller are spheres that slowly arc through the air. We want to better approximate the fast-moving bullets that we are used to in traditional shooters.

To change the properties of the projectile, we need to open the Blueprint called `FirstPersonProjectile`, located in the same `Blueprints` folder as `FirstPersonCharacter`. Once opened, look at the **Components** panel and click on **Projectile**. This is a projectile movement component that has been added onto our sphere mesh and collider to define how the sphere will travel once it is created in the world.

In the **Details** panel, you will see that **Projectile** is made up of a long series of values that can be modified relative to movement. We are interested in only a couple of these at this time:

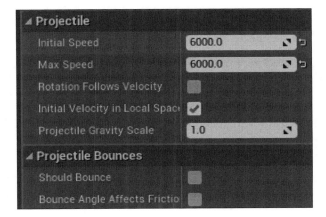

First, find the **Initial Speed** and **Max Speed** fields, currently set to 3000. The initial speed determines how fast the projectile travels when it is first created at the tip of our gun, and the maximum speed determines how fast it can reach if an additional force is applied to it after creation. If we had a rocket, we might wish to apply acceleration to the rocket after it is launched to signify the thruster engaging. However, since we are representing a bullet coming from a gun, it makes more sense to make its initial speed the fastest that the bullet will ever travel at. Adjust both the initial speed and the maximum speed to twice their original value, 6000.

Additionally, you might have noticed that the current projectile bounces off walls and objects as if it were a rubber ball. However, we want to mimic a harder and more forcefully impacting projectile. To remove the bouncing, look for the **Projectile Bounces** section in the **Details** panel and uncheck the box next to **Should Bounce**. The other values dictate the way in which the projectile bounces only if **Should Bounce** is checked, so there is no need to adjust them.

Now compile, save, and click on **Play**. You will find that shooting the gun results in a much further reaching projectile, which behaves more like bullet.

Adding sound and particle effects

Now that we have the player moving and shooting to our liking, let's turn our attention to the enemy targets. Shooting one of the target cylinders currently results in it changing its color to red. However, there is nothing that the player can currently do to destroy a target outright.

We can add more dynamics to our enemy interaction by producing Blueprint logic that destroys the target if it is shot more than once, while increasing the reward for the player by producing a satisfying sound and visual effect once the target is destroyed.

Giving our targets state with branches

Since we want to generate effects that will be caused by changes in state applied to our target cylinder, we have to ensure that this logic is contained within our CylinderTarget Blueprint. Open the Blueprint from your Blueprints folder, and take a look at the node group that triggers off of **Event Hit**. Right now, when our projectile hits the cylinder object, these nodes tell it to swap to a red material. To add the ability to change how the cylinder behaves when it is shot more than once, we will need to add a check to our Blueprints to count the number of times the cylinder has been hit, and then trigger a different result, depending on its state.

Let's take a look at a setup that could help us handle this scenario:

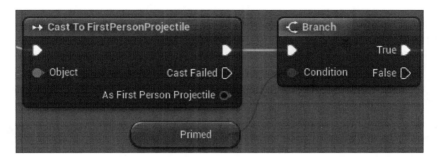

To create conditional logic with multiple outcomes in Blueprints, we are taking advantage of the **Branch** node. This node takes a Boolean variable as an input. Since Boolean values can only be either true or false, the **Branch** node can produce only two outcomes. These two outcomes can be executed by linking additional nodes to the two output execution pins, representing the true path and the false path.

The first step of creating a branch is to determine what will be represented by your Boolean, and what will cause the conditional value to change from false to true. In our case, we want to create a primed state that shows that the target has been hit, and that it could be destroyed with a second hit. Let's go ahead and create a `Primed` Boolean variable.

Recall that variables are defined in the **My Blueprint** panel. You should already see our previously defined variables for speed and direction. Click on the **+** button to add a new variable. New variables are automatically created as Booleans, so there is no need to change the variable type in this case. Give it the name `Primed` and check the box labeled **Editable** to make this value easier to modify externally. Finally, compile and save the Blueprint. Because we do not want our targets to be in a primed state before they have been hit for the first time, we will leave the default value of our variable to false (represented by an unchecked box).

Now that you have a `Primed` Boolean variable, drag it from the **My Blueprint** panel to the event graph, and select the **Get** option that appears on release. This will grab the true or false state data from the variable and enable us to use it to branch our Blueprints. Click and drag a red wire from the output pin of the new **Primed** node to empty space on the event graph. Search for and add the **Branch** node.

Finally, we can add the branch to our **Event Hit** Blueprint group. Break the connection between the **Cast ToFirstPersonProjectile** and **Set Material** nodes by holding down the *Alt* key and clicking on one of the execution pins. Drag the **Set Material** node out of the way for a moment, and then connect the output execution pin to the input execution pin of the **Branch** node. This Blueprint will now call the branch evaluation every time the target cylinder is hit.

Now that we have our Branch node set up for activation, we need to provide the target cylinder with instructions on what to do in each state. The targets we want to create can be described as being in one of these three states at any time: **Default**, **Primed**, and **Destroyed**. Since a destroyed actor can't execute any behavior, there is no way to develop any behavior that happens *after* the target is destroyed. As a consequence, we really have to concern ourselves with only the primed and the pre-primed default states.

Let's handle the default state first. Since this branch dictates what happens to the cylinder in each state *after* it has been hit, we want to execute the material change that we previously attached to the event. If the target has not yet been hit, and it is now hit for the first time, we have to change the material to red. Additionally, we will also have to set our Primed Boolean variable to **True**. In this way, when the target is hit again, the branch node will route the behavior to the other execution sequence. The **False** execution sequence of nodes will look like this:

Drag the **Set Material** node you moved aside before to the right of the **Branch** node, and then connect the **False** output execution pin of the **Branch** node to the **Set Material** node's input execution pin. Now drag the Primed variable from the **My Blueprint** panel to the event graph, and select the **Set** option. Connect this node to the **Set Material** node's output execution pin, and click on the checkbox next to **Primed** within the **Set** node. This will ensure that the next time the target is hit, the branch evaluates to true.

Triggering sound effects, explosions, and destruction

The next step is to define the sequence of actions that will be triggered from the **True** path of the **Branch** node. Earlier, we identified three things we wanted to accomplish when destroying a target. These were hearing an explosion, seeing an explosion, and actually removing the target object from the game world. We'll start with the often undervalued, but always critical, element of satisfying game experiences — sound.

The most basic interaction we can design with sound is to play a `.wav` sound file at a location in the game world once, and this will work perfectly for our purpose. Drag a wire from the **True** execution node of the **Branch** node to empty grid space, and search for the **Play Sound at Location** node:

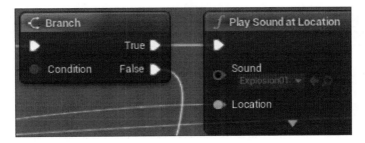

Play Sound at Location is a simple node that takes a sound file input and a location input, and — as you might have guessed — plays the sound at that location. There are several sound files included in the default assets we brought into this project, and you can see the list of these by clicking on the drop-down menu underneath the **Sound** input. Find and select **Explosion01** to set an explosion sound effect.

Now that we have set the sound, we need to determine where the sound will play. We can use a process similar to the one we used to set the field of view by taking the mesh component of the cylinder target, extracting its location value, and then linking that location vector directly to our sound node. However, the **Event Hit** trigger will make it easier on us.

One of the many output pins on the **Event Hit** node is called **Hit Location**. This pin contains the location in space where the two objects evaluated by **Event Hit** are colliding with one another. The location of our projectile hitting the target is a perfectly reasonable place to generate the explosion effect, so go ahead and drag a wire from **Hit Location** on the **Event Hit** node to the **Location** input pin on **Play Sound at Location**.

Compile, save, and play to test Blueprint. Shooting one of the moving targets once will turn it red. Every hit after that should produce an explosion sound effect.

Now that we have the sound of our explosion working, let's add the visual effect and destroy the cylinder, using the following setup:

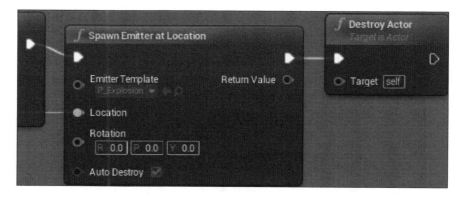

Drag a wire from the output execution node of **Play Sound at Location** to empty grid space. Search for and select the **Spawn Emitter at Location** node.

An **emitter** is an object that will produce particle effects in a particular location. Particle effects are collections of small objects that combine to create the visual effect of objects that are fluid, gaseous, or otherwise intangible, such as waterfall impacts, explosions, or light beams.

The **Spawn Emitter at Location** node looks similar to the sound node we are attaching it to, except for the additional rotation input and the **Auto Destroy** toggle. In the drop-down menu beneath **Emitter Template**, find and select the **P_Explosion** effect. This is another asset that came packed with the standard assets we pulled into our project, and will produce a satisfying-looking explosion wherever its emitter is attached.

Since we want the explosion to be generated in the same location as the sound of explosion, we click and drag the same **Hit Location** pin of the **Event Hit** node over into the **Location** pin of **Spawn Emitter at Location**. The explosion is a three-dimensional effect that looks the same from all angles, so we can leave the **Rotation** input alone. The toggle for **Auto Destroy** determines whether or not the emitter can be triggered more than once. We will be destroying the actor that contains this emitter once this particle effect is created, so we can leave the toggle box checked.

Finally, we want to remove the target cylinder from the game world after the sound and visual explosion effects are played. Drag the output execution pin from the **Spawn Emitter at Location** node and drop it into empty grid space. To find the **Destroy Actor** node, you will need to uncheck the **Context Sensitive** checkbox temporarily. Do so and then search for and add the **Destroy Actor** node. This node takes only a single target input, which defaults to **self**. Since this Blueprint contains the cylinder objects we want to destroy and **self** is exactly what we want to destroy, we can leave this node as is.

Extend the comment box around the entire **Event Hit** sequence of nodes, and update the text to describe what the new sequence accomplishes. I chose `When hit, turn red and set to primed. If already primed, destroy self`. The final result of this chain of Blueprints should look something like what is shown in the following screenshot:

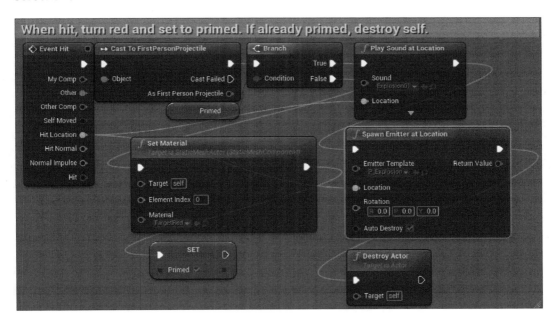

Once you have left a useful comment around the Blueprint nodes, compile, save, and click on **Play** to test the new interactions. You should see and hear the cylinders explode once they have been shot two times by the player's gun.

Summary

We've now started going down the path to making our game feel satisfying to the player. We have sound and visual effects, a player character that has most of the capabilities we would expect from a modern shooter, and targets that react to the player's interactions. The skills we have covered in the first two chapters can already be combined to start creating increasingly complex and interesting behavior.

In this chapter, we created some customized player controls to allow sprinting and zooming in with our gun. In the process, you explored how the movement controller translates information from a player's inputs into the game experience. You also opened the door to creating simple animations using timelines. Then you added more feedback to the player's interaction with the environment by attaching an explosion effect and sound to the enemy targets, and adding another requirement for them to be hit by two projectiles.

In the next chapter, we will explore adding a user interface to our game to provide the player with feedback on their state relative to the world.

3
Creating Screen UI Elements

At the core of any game experience is the method the game designers use to communicate the goals and rules of the game to the player. One method of doing this, which is common across all forms of games, is through the use of a **Graphical User Interface (GUI)** to display and broadcast important information to the player. In this chapter, we will be setting up a GUI that will track the player's health, stamina, and ammo, and we will set up a counter that will display the objectives to the player. You will learn how to set up a basic user interface using Unreal's GUI editor and how to use Blueprints to tie that interface to gameplay values. We will create UI elements using the **Unreal Motion Graphics UI Designer (UMG)**. In the process, we will cover the following topics:

- Creating UI elements using UMG
  - Drawing UI elements with the widget designer
  - Setting up Blueprints to display the GUI
- Creating widget Blueprints to modify the values displayed on the GUI
  - Creating variables to track the player's state with the UI
  - Retrieving variables to change the UI's appearance

Creating simple UI meters with UMG

To create an **HUD** (short for **Heads-up Display**) that will display the amount of health, stamina, and ammo the player currently possesses, we will first need to create variables within the player character that can track these values. To do so, open the **FirstPersonCharacter** Blueprint from the `Blueprints` folder of your project. Within the Blueprint, we are going to define variables that will represent additional states that the player and game will care about. Find the **Variables** category of the **My Blueprint** panel in the editor. Click on the **+** sign to add another variable, and call it `PlayerHealth`. With **PlayerHealth** selected, find the **Details** panel and change the variable type to **Float**.

Also ensure that the box labeled **Editable** is checked so that other Blueprints and objects can manipulate this variable. When a variable is made editable, it will be shown with a yellow open eye symbol next to its name in the **Variables** section of the **My Blueprint** panel.

Follow the same steps again in order to create a second float variable called PlayerStamina. Next, create a third variable, but this time select the **Integer** variable type, labeled as **Int**, and call it PlayerCurrentAmmo. Finally, create a second **Int** variable called **TargetKillCount**. The final result of the player variables should look like what is shown in the following screenshot:

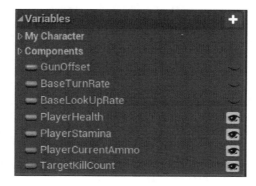

Now, we need to set the default values of our three new variables. We can do so by clicking on each of these variables and changing the field under **Default Value** in the **Details** panel. I set **PlayerCurrentAmmo** to 30 and **TargetKillCount** to 0, but you can tweak the default values to whatever you think is appropriate for your desired game experience at any time. **PlayerHealth** and **PlayerStamina** should both be set to 1, as we will be representing those with UI meters that will display the degree of fullness between 0 and 1. Once you have set the defaults, compile and save your Blueprint.

Drawing shapes with widget Blueprints

Since the First Person template has no user interface elements by default, we should create a new folder to store our GUI work. Return to the **FirstPersonExampleMap** tab and navigate to the **Content Browser** panel. Open the FirstPersonBP folder, right-click in empty space next to the list of folders, and select the **New Folder** option. Let's keep things simple and call this folder UI.

Open the UI folder you just made, and right-click in empty folder space. Go to **User Interface | Widget Blueprint** and name the resulting Blueprint HUD. Double-click on this Blueprint to open the UMG editor. We will be using this tool to define how our UI is going to look on the screen.

Within the UMG editor, find the panel labeled **Palette**. Inside it, open the category named **Panel**. You will see a series of containers listed that can organize the UI information. The one we are looking for is called **Horizontal Box**. Select and drag a **Horizontal Box** out of the **Palette** panel onto the **Hierarchy** panel, releasing it on top of the **[CanvasPanel]** object.

You should now see a horizontal box object nested underneath the **[Canvas Panel]** object in the hierarchy. Our immediate goal is to create two labeled player stats bars, using a combination of vertical boxes, text, and progress bars. The final setup will look like this:

Two vertical boxes will contain the text and progress bars of our player stats UI. Look again at the **Panel** category within the **Palette** panel, and drag the **Vertical Box** object onto the **Horizontal Box** you created in **Hierarchy**. Do this a second time, so that two vertical boxes are aligned underneath the horizontal box.

To keep things organized, let's apply labels to our objects. Click on the horizontal box and look at the **Details** panel on the right side of the editor. Change the top field, which shows the label of the horizontal box, to say Player Stats.

Using the same method, change the labels of the two vertical boxes underneath **Player Stats** to **Player Stats Text** and **Player Stats Bars**. Now look under the **Common** category of the **Palette** panel to find the textboxes and progress bars we need to create the UI. Drag two **Text** objects onto your **Player Stats Text** object, and two **Progress Bar** objects onto **Player Stats Bars**.

Customizing the meter's appearance

Now we want to adjust the UI elements and place them on the screen. Select the **Player Stats** object from the hierarchy, and look at the central graph panel. You will see some size controls that allow you to manipulate the size of the selected objects. Resize the elements so that you can see two sets of the words **Text Block** and two tiny gray progress bars stacked on top of each other.

The large rectangular outline in the graph view represents the boundaries of the screen that the player will see, called the **canvas**. This is the **[CanvasPanel]** object seen at the top level of the hierarchy. Elements positioned toward the top-left corner of the canvas will appear in the top-left corner of the in-game screen. Since we want our health and stamina bars to appear in the top-left corner, make sure that the **Player Stats** object is still selected and move the entire group close to, but not touching, the top-left corner of the canvas.

Next, take a look at the **Hierarchy** panel again. Select the top progress bar underneath **Player Stats** bars. In the **Details** panel, change the top label field to Health Bar. Then find the **Size** toggle under the **Slot** category, and click on the **Fill** button to adjust the vertical height of the bar. Finally, find **Fill Color** and **Opacity** under **Appearance**, and set the color to a shade of red.

Now let's repeat this operation for the player's stamina. Click on the second progress bar. In the **Details** panel, click on the **Fill** button and set the progress bar's label to Stamina Bar. Find **Fill Color** and **Opacity** and adjust the color to something that looks green. Finally, click on the **Player Stats** bars vertical box, and then on the **Fill** button there as well to scale the horizontal size of both the bars.

We have our meters looking as we expect, so now let's adjust the text labels. Click on the first text bar underneath **Player Stats Text** in the **Hierarchy** panel. Change its label to Health, and click on the **Align Right** button next to **Horizontal Align** to position the text against the bar. If you wish to change the font size or style, you can adjust it from the **Font** dropdowns and fields underneath the **Appearance** category. After you have adjusted **Health**, click on the second textbox object. Label this one Stamina, click on the **Align Right** button, and adjust the font size and style to your liking:

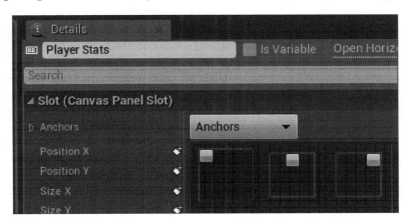

The final bit of adjustment to make is to anchor the meters to a side of the screen. Since screen sizes and ratios can vary, we want to ensure that our UI elements remain in the same relative position on the screen. **Anchors** are used to define a widget's desired position on a canvas, regardless of the screen size. To establish an anchor for our meters, select the **Player Stats** top-level object and then click on the **Anchors** dropdown on the **Details** panel. Select the first option that appears, which shows a gray rectangle in the top-left corner of the screen. This will anchor our meters to that corner, ensuring that they will always appear in the top-left corner, regardless of the resolution or ratio. If you desire to add more nuances to the anchors, you can click on the expansion arrow to the left of the word **Anchors** to expose the precision transform controls. Using this, you will have the ability to anchor an object to any point on the canvas. You can also accomplish the same effect by dragging the eight-leaved white flower shape that appears when you set an anchor at the location where you would like the anchor to be on the canvas.

You can now adjust the size and position of the **Player Stats** group of objects within the **Canvas** panel to mimic how you want them to appear in your game. The final product should appear something like this:

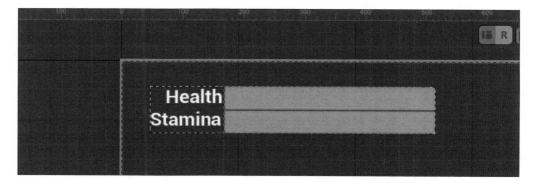

Creating ammo and enemy counters

Now that we have a display for the player stats, let's work on our ammo counter and gameplay goal displays. Both of these will work similarly to our player stats meters, except that we want to represent their values through text rather than a continuous meter.

To begin the setup, drag two additional **Horizontal Box** objects down from **Palette** to the **[CanvasPanel]** object in the **Hierarchy** panel. Rename these horizontal boxes to Weapon Stats and Goal Tracker by clicking on the box and changing the top field in the **Details** panel that appears.

Now drag two **Text** objects onto **Weapon Stats**. Select the first text object, and change both its name and the **Text** value under **Content** to be Ammo :, including the space and colon. In order to ensure that the size of this display matches the meter text, change the font size to 24. You can leave all other values untouched, for now.

Next, select the second text object and change its name to Ammo Left. This value is going to change as ammo is used, but we should give it some default. Since we set the default of our ammo variable on the player Blueprint to be 30, go ahead and change the **Text** value of **Ammo Left** to 30 as well.

Finally, let's adjust the position of our ammo tracker. Click on the **Weapon Stats** object, and then drag the box on the graph panel toward the top-right corner of the canvas. You will need to resize the box until **Ammo : 30** can be fully seen inside the containing box. The last step will be to set the anchors on the **Weapon Stats** object in the top-right corner, which is the third option provided in the **Anchors** dropdown in the **Details** panel.

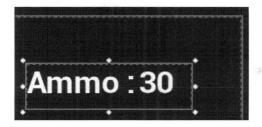

We can now replicate this procedure for the goal tracker. Drag two additional **Text** objects onto the **Goal Tracker** object in the hierarchy. Change the first text object's name and **Text** value to be `Targets Eliminated :`. Label the second text object `Target Count` and set its text value to a default of `0`.

Knowing what goal the player is working against is one of the most important pieces of information that a game can convey. We can reflect this by giving our goal tracker a larger font size than the rest of the UI. Set the font size of both text objects to `32` to give the goal tracker more prominence on the screen.

Finally, adjust the size and position of the **Goal Tracker** object so that all of the text can be seen and is positioned in the top center of the **Canvas** panel. Leave a little additional space to the right side of `0` so that the goal tracker container has room to display multiple-digit numbers. Then set the anchor point of **Goal Tracker** to be in the top center by selecting the second option from the **Anchors** drop-down menu.

With the UI elements aligned the way we want them, you now need to ensure that the game will actually know how to display the HUD. To do this, we will need to revisit the character Blueprint.

Displaying the HUD

Return to the **FirstPersonExampleMap** tab and **Content Browser**. Find and open the **FirstPersonCharacter** Blueprint in the `Blueprints` folder. In the event graph, right-click in empty space, search for **EventBeginPlay**, and place the trigger.

In most cases, **EventBeginPlay** will call the subsequent actions as soon as the game is started. If the actor the Blueprint is attached to isn't present when the game starts, it will instead trigger as soon as the actor is spawned. Since the **FirstPersonCharacter** player object is present as soon as the game begins, attaching our Blueprint logic to this trigger will spawn the HUD immediately.

Drag a wire from the output execution pin of **EventBeginPlay**, and add a **CreateWidget** node. Within the node, you will see a drop-down menu labeled **Class**. Here is our opportunity to link in the widget Blueprint we created. Recall that you called this widget HUD. Sure enough, if you open the drop-down menu, you will see the **HUD** option available. Select it to have the player character Blueprint generate the UI elements you created.

Although we now have a widget generated when the game starts, there is a final step required to get the widget containing our UI elements to actually appear on the screen. Drag the **Return Value** output pin into empty grid space, and add an **Add to Viewport** node. This will link the widget information to the display the player sees when interacting with the game. The output execution pin should automatically connect with the new node, completing our Blueprint chain. Remember to create a comment for yourself around the three nodes. The final product should appear as follows:

Now compile, save, and click on **Play** to test the game. You should see the two meters representing the player's health and stamina, as well as numerical counters for ammo and eliminated targets. But as you shoot from your gun, you may notice one very important problem—none of the UI values change! We will be addressing this missing component in the next section.

Connecting UI values to player variables

To allow our UI elements to pull data from our player variables, we will need to revisit the HUD widget Blueprint. Navigate to the **FirstPersonExampleMap** tab, go to the **Content Browser** panel, and open the HUD widget Blueprint in the UI folder.

Creating bindings for health and stamina

In order to get our UI to update with the player stats, we will be creating a **binding**. Bindings give the ability to tie functions or properties of a Blueprint to a widget. Whenever the property or function is updated, that change is reflected in the widget automatically. So, instead of manually updating both the player health stat and our widget every time the player takes damage (so that the health meter display changes), we can tie the meter to a player value—health. Then only one value needs to be updated.

In the HUD Blueprint editor, find the **Hierarchy** panel and click on the **Health Bar** object nested underneath the **Player Stats Bars** object. With the **Health Bar** now selected, locate the **Percent** field in the **Appearance** category of the **Details** panel. Click on the **Bind** button next to **Percent**, and select **Create Binding**, as shown in this screenshot:

The HUD editor will switch from **Designer View** to **Graph View**. A new function has been created, allowing us to script a connection between the meter and the player's health variable. Right-click in empty graph space, and add a **Get Player Character** node. Drag a wire from the **Return Value** output pin of the new node to empty space, and add the **Cast to FirstPersonCharacter** node. Break the execution pin connection between the **Get Health Bar Percent** and **ReturnNode** nodes, and instead connect **Get Health Bar Percent** to our casting node, as shown here:

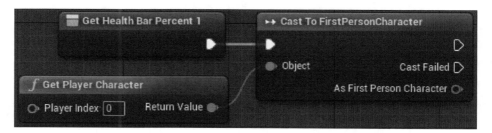

 This combination of nodes retrieves the player character object for use within the HUD Blueprint. However, any custom functions or variables we created for the player character in the FirstPersonCharacter Blueprint will remain off limits until we cast the player character object to the FirstPersonCharacter Blueprint. Remember that casting works to check and ensure that the input object is the specific object you are casting to. So, the preceding combination of nodes is essentially saying: *if the player character is a FirstPersonCharacter, allow me to access the FirstPersonCharacter functions and variables tied to that player character.*

Next, drag a wire from the **As First Person Character** output pin to empty grid space, and add a **Get Player Health** node. Finally, connect the **Cast to FirstPersonCharacter** node execution pin to **ReturnNode**, as shown in the following screenshot:

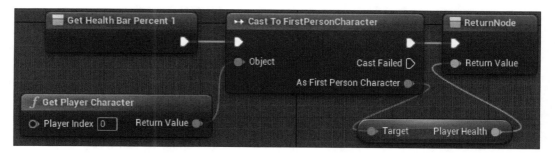

That's all we need to do to connect the player health to the UI health bar. We need to follow the same operation for the player stamina. Click on the large button labeled **Designer** to return to the **Canvas** view, and then select **Stamina Bar** in the **Hierarchy** panel. By following the steps outlined previously for the health bar, create a binding that connects the **FirstPersonCharacter** variable **Player Stamina** to the meter.

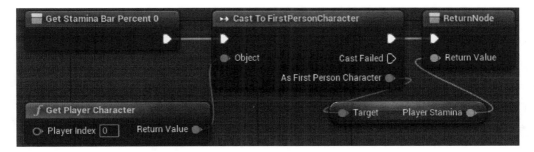

Compile and save your work. If you click on **Play**, you will now notice that the health and stamina meters are filled in with red and green bars respectively. The next step is to hook up our bindings for the ammo count and goal counters.

Making text bindings

Click on the **Designer** button to return to the **Canvas** interface once more. This time, we want to select the **Ammo Left** text object in the hierarchy, under **Weapon Stats**. In the **Details** panel, find the **Bind** button next to the **Text** field, and create a new binding, as shown here:

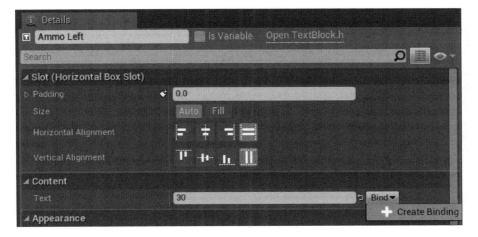

We will follow the same pattern for this binding as we did for health and stamina. In the **Get Ammo Left Text** graph view that appears, create a **Get Player Character** node, cast it to the **FirstPersonCharacter** node, and then link the **As First Person Character** pin to **Get Player Current Ammo**. Finally, attach both the cast node and the **Get Player Current Ammo** node to **ReturnNode**. You will notice that when you attach the **Player Current Ammo** output pin to the **Return Value** input pin, a new **To Text (Int)** node will be created and linked automatically. This is because the Unreal Engine knows that for you to display a numerical value as text on the screen, it first needs to convert the number into a text format that the widget knows how to display. The conversion node will be hooked up already, so there is no need to make further modifications:

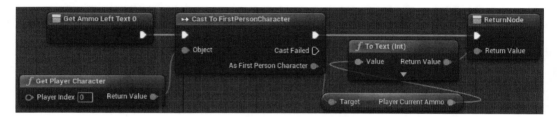

The final binding to create is for our goal tracker target count. Return to the **Designer** view and select the **Target Count** object in the hierarchy under **Goal Tracker**. Click on the **Bind** button next to the **Text** field in the **Display** panel. By following the preceding steps, create a Blueprint chain that grabs the player character, casts it to **FirstPersonCharacter**, and connects the **Target Kill Count** variable to the casting and return nodes. As with the ammo count, the conversion to a text node will be automatically generated and connected for you. The final result should look like what is shown in the following screenshot:

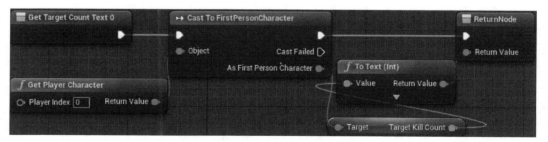

We've now successfully bound all our UI elements to player variables. Now is a good time to compile and save our work. Because of our bindings, the UI will now do its job of responding to events that occur within our game. However, we still need to create the events that will trigger changes in the variables we have connected. In the next section, we will be modifying the player variables based on actions that the player takes while playing.

Tracking the ammo and eliminated targets

To get our UI to respond to the player interacting with the environment, we will need to modify the Blueprint scripting that controls the player and targets. To begin, let's get the ammo counter to decrease when the player fires a shot from their gun.

Reducing the ammo counter

The Blueprints managing the firing of the player's gun are contained within the `FirstPersonCharacter` Blueprint. Find this Blueprint within the `Blueprints` folder of **Content Browser** and open it. Now find the large series of Blueprint nodes contained within the comment block **Spawn projectile**. We want to ensure that the counter tracking the player's current ammo count reduces by one, each time the player fires a shot. The Blueprint scripting required to do so looks like this:

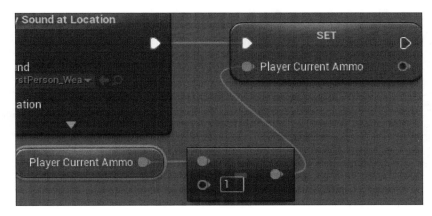

Find the final node in the chain, **Play Sound at Location**. Drag a wire from the output execution pin of this node to empty grid space, and add a **Set Player Current Ammo** node. Then drag a wire from the **Player Current Ammo** input pin to empty space, and create an **Int – Int** node. Next, drag a wire from the top input pin of this node out and add a **Get Player Current Ammo** node. Finally, fill in the bottom field of the **Int – Int** node with 1. This sequence translates to: *after firing a sound, set the player's current ammo count to the existing ammo count minus one*. Compile, save, and play to see your ammo counter decrease every time you fire a shot from your gun.

Increasing the targets eliminated counter

Next, we want to increase our targets eliminated counter by 1 every time a target cylinder is destroyed. Recall that the Blueprint scripting that controlled the destruction of the cylinder targets was attached to the `CylinderTarget_Blueprint` Blueprint. Open this Blueprint, which is contained inside the `Blueprints` folder of **Content Browser**.

There is only one chain of Blueprint nodes inside this Blueprint, all being triggered by **Event Hit**. We will have to add our new nodes close to the end of this chain, after all nodes except **Destroy Actor**. Break the link between the **Spawn Emitter at Location** and **Destroy Actor** nodes, and then move **Destroy Actor** to the right to give plenty of room for our new Blueprint scripting. The goal is to create a series of nodes that will extract the current target kill count from the player character, and increase it by one before going on to destroy the actor. The end result will look like what is shown in the following screenshot:

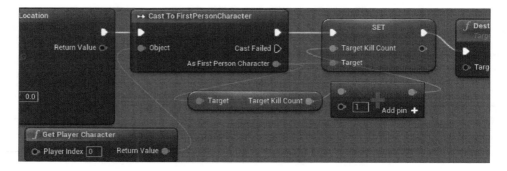

Target Kill Count is a variable of the **FirstPersonCharacter** Blueprint, so just as we did when we created our bindings earlier in the chapter, we will need to get the player character object and cast it to **FirstPersonCharacter**. Add a **Get Player Character** node, and then connect its **Return Value** pin to a **Cast to FirstPersonCharacter** node.

Now drag a wire from the **As First Person Character** pin to empty grid space, and add a **Get Target Kill Count** node. From that node's output pin, create an **Int + Int** node, changing the bottom field to 1. Next, drag this new node's output pin into empty space and create a **Set Target Kill Count** node. Additionally, you will have to drag a wire from the casting node's **As First Person Character** output pin to the **Target** input pin of the **Set Target Kill Count** node. Finally, connect the execution pins of the **Cast to FirstPersonCharacter**, **Set Target Kill Count**, and **Destroy Actor** nodes, ensuring that **Destroy Actor** is the final node in the chain. Compile, save, and play the game to see the targets eliminated counter on the screen increase every time you destroy a target cylinder:

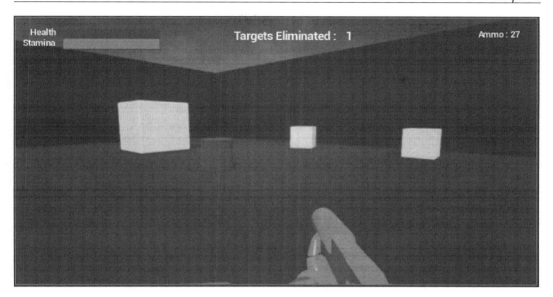

Summary

In this chapter, we enhanced player experience by adding a HUD that tracks the player's interaction with the environment. In doing so, you developed another conduit through which you can communicate information to the player of your game. By now, we have the skeletal structure of a first-person shooter, including guns that shoot, targets that explode, and a UI that exposes the state of the world to the player. We have already come a long way from the initial test scene, which featured minimal player interaction.

In the next chapter, we will begin transitioning from building the foundation of our game structure to constructing the design of our game. The core of any game is made up of the rules that the player must follow in order to create a fun experience. While the game in its current form features some basic rules that define how the targets react on being shot, the overall experience lacks a goal for the player to achieve. We will be rectifying this by establishing a win condition for the player, as well as providing additional constraints that make the experience holistic and consistent.

4
Creating Constraints and Gameplay Objectives

In this chapter, we'll be defining a rule set for our game, which will guide the player through the play experience. We want to give the player the ability to start the game and immediately identify what they have to do in order to win the game. In its most basic form, a game could be defined by the win condition and the steps the player can take to reach that win condition. Ideally, we want to ensure that each step the player takes toward that goal is fun.

We'll begin by applying some constraints to the player in order to increase the level of difficulty. A game without challenge quickly becomes boring, and we want to ensure that every mechanic in our game is providing the player with an interesting choice or challenge. We'll then set up a goal for the player to achieve, along with the necessary adjustments to our enemy targets to make that goal a challenge to reach. In this process, we'll work to accomplish the following:

- Reducing stamina while the player is sprinting
- Preventing the player's gun from firing if they run out of ammo
- Creating ammo pickups that allow the player to regain ammo
- Defining a win condition based on the number of targets eliminated
- Creating a menu that allows the player to replay or quit the game upon winning

Constraining player actions

One important consideration to make when adding enhanced capabilities to the player is the impact that the ability had on both the challenge and feel of the game experience. Recall that we added the ability for the player to sprint in the last chapter by holding down the *Shift* key. As it currently stands, holding down the *Shift* key while moving provides a significant increase in the speed at which the player can move. Without constraints applied to this ability, such as an enforced waiting period between uses, there would be nothing discouraging the player from holding down the *Shift* key at all times as they move.

This goes against the goal we set out to accomplish by adding sprint functionality, which was to provide more options to the player. If an option is so attractive that the player feels compelled to utilize it at all times, it doesn't actually increase the number of interesting choices available to the player. From the player's perspective, the result would be the same if we just increased the base speed of the player to the sprint speed.

We can rectify this and other issues currently faced by our game prototype by adding constraints that limit player abilities to increase decision making.

Draining stamina while sprinting

To add a constraint to the sprinting ability of the player, we'll need to return to the Blueprint where we originally defined the ability. Open the **FirstPersonCharacter** Blueprint located in the `Blueprints` folder of the **Content Browser**.

First, we need to create a couple of variables that will keep track of whether or not the player is sprinting and how much sprinting should cost. Find the **Variables** category of the **My Blueprint** panel and click the **+** button twice to add two new variables. Rename the first variable to `SprintCost` and assign it the type **Float**. Make sure to click the checkbox next to **Editable** as true and set the variable's default value to `0.1`. Rename the second variable to `IsSprinting?`. Set the variable type to **Boolean** and make the variable editable. After compiling the Blueprint, find some empty graph space near the block of Blueprint nodes you created for the sprint function, which should have a comment block labeled **Sprint** around it.

We are going to create a **custom event** to drain the player's stamina at a consistent rate while they are sprinting. A custom event allows us to trigger the Blueprints that are attached to the event whenever another Blueprint calls that event. In this way, groups of Blueprint nodes within the same Blueprint can communicate with one another, even when they are not connected directly:

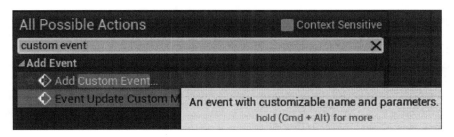

Search for a **Custom Event** node and add it, putting it a moderate distance away from your other sprint nodes. When you add a **Custom Event** node, look at the **Details** panel and find the **Name** field. This allows you to create the name of your custom function. The name you give to the custom event is important as you will be establishing the name by which the function will be referenced by the function calls that trigger it. In this case, let's call the function Sprint Drain. Type Sprint Drain into the **Name** field and press the **Enter** key to establish the event. The Blueprint structure we'll be following for this sequence looks like the following screenshot:

First, drag a wire from the **Sprint Drain** event onto empty grid space and add a **Set Player Stamina** node. Next, attach the **Player Stamina** input pin to a **Max (Float)** node. This node will output the highest of the float numbers given as inputs. We want to ensure that the player stamina never dips below 0, so leave the bottom pin at 0.0 and drag a wire from the top input pin of this node and attach it to a **Float – Float** node. To the top input pin of the **Float – Float** node, attach a **Get Player Stamina** node. In the bottom pin, we'll establish the amount of stamina to drain while sprinting.

We could enter a number into the field next to the bottom input pin of this node. However, if we ever wished to change the amount of stamina drained by sprinting, we would need to open this Blueprint, find this node, and adjust the value within this small text box each time. A better habit to get into is to use a custom, public variable that we attach to this pin, which will allow us to tweak the amount of stamina drain incurred by sprinting continually, without even entering the Blueprint editor interface. Because we already created variables for both sprint cost and checking if the player is sprinting, we'll use the sprint cost variable here. Either drag the **SprintCost** variable onto the bottom input pin of **Float – Float**, or drag a wire from the bottom pin out and search for **Get SprintCost**.

Next, we want to stop both the sprint and the stamina drain effect when the player runs out of stamina. Drag a wire from the output execution pin of the **Set Player Stamina** node and attach it to a **Branch** node. Now drag a wire from the **Condition** input pin of this node and attach it to a **Float >= Float** node. Drag a second wire from the **Get Player Stamina** node onto the top input pin of the **Float >= Float** node and drag a second wire from the **Get Sprint Cost** node to the bottom input pin. This will determine whether or not the player has enough stamina to continue sprinting.

In the event that the player does not have enough stamina to take another tick of stamina draining sprinting, we need to force the player back to a walk speed and clear the timer that will be calling this custom function. Do so by dragging the **CharacterMovement** component down from the **Components** panel and drop it near the **Branch** node. Drag a wire from this node and attach it to a **Set Max Walk Speed** node. Set the **Max Walk Speed** field to 600 to match the default walk speed we established. Now, connect the input execution pin of this node to the **False** output execution pin of the **Branch** node.

Next, drag a wire from the **Set Max Walk Speed** node's output execution pin and attach it to a **Clear Timer** node. Type in Sprint Drain precisely into the **Function Name** input field to link it to the custom event. Finally, attach a **Set Is Sprinting?** node to the output execution pin of **Clear Timer**, ensuring that the checkbox is left unchecked.

Now select all five nodes and create a comment around them explaining their utility for draining the player's stamina. I chose **Sprinting Drains Stamina by Sprint Cost**. The next step will be to call our new custom event from inside the Blueprint nodes that manage our sprint. Remember to compile and save the Blueprint.

Using looping timers to repeat actions

Now, we want to customize our sprint Blueprint nodes to fire the custom event that we just created so that the player's stamina drains as they sprint., as seen in the following screenshot:

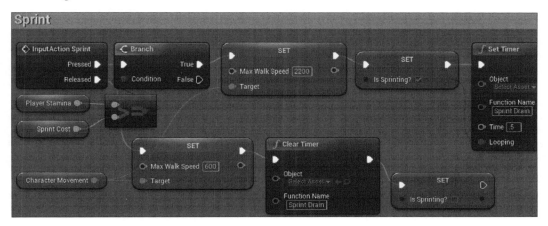

From the output execution pin of the node setting walk speed to 2200, drag a wire onto empty space and add a **Set Is Sprinting?** node. Check the checkbox inside this node to set the **Boolean** to true when the player is sprinting. Next, we want to make sure that stamina is continually drained as long as the left *Shift* key is held down. To do so, we can utilize a timer, as shown in the following screenshot:

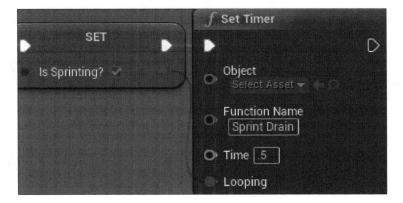

Timers allow us to perform an action after a designated amount of time has expired or even fire an action repeatedly on a set time interval. It is this second functionality that is going to serve the purpose of looping our sprint drain function repeatedly.

Drag a wire from the execution output pin of the **Set Is Sprinting?** node onto empty graph space and add a **Set Timer** node. Inside this node, click on the field underneath the label **Function Name**, and type in Sprint Drain to connect the timer to our custom event.

The second input we want to adjust in the timer node is labeled **Time**, which will determine the interval at which our sprint draining event is triggered. Put .5 into the **Time** field to give the draining effect a notable, steady default rate. If you expect that you might want to tweak this value repeatedly, you could also choose to create a custom float variable and attach that to this input instead, in a way similar to how we handled SprintCost. Finally, drag a wire from the red output pin of the **Set Is Sprinting?** node and attach it to the **Looping** input pin to ensure that Sprint Drain is called repeatedly at each time interval as long as the **Is Sprinting?** Boolean is set to true.

With this completed, this function will now ensure that the value we designated for the SprintCost variable will be drained from the player stamina meter every .5 seconds, starting when the left *Shift* key is pressed as long as the player is sprinting. However, we want the drain effect to stop when the player stops sprinting by letting go of the key. To accomplish this, we need to stop the timer using **Clear Timer**, just as we did inside the Sprint Drain function.

Attach a **Clear Timer** node to the output execution node of the **Set Max Walk Speed** node attached to the **Left Shift** node's **Released** output pin. This node will abort out of the timer attached to the function name given. Type in Sprint Drain into the **Function Name** field of this node to link the node to the timer node we just made. End this sequence by attaching a **Set Is Sprinting?** node to the output execution pin of **Clear Timer** and leave the checkbox unchecked.

As an alternative to **Clear Timer**, you could use the node **Pause Timer**. Pausing the timer works almost identically, except that the remaining time on the timer countdown before it was paused would persist when the timer is activated again. So if you paused a ten second timer that had five seconds left until the next activation, the attached function would trigger next after five seconds instead of ten at next activation.

Compile, save, and test the game. As you sprint around the level, you should see your stamina meter deplete in regular increments while the left *Shift* key is held down. The next step to constrain sprinting is to ensure that the player cannot initiate a sprint if they are drained of stamina.

Blocking actions with branches

Preventing the player from sprinting when they don't have sufficient stamina can be accomplished by adding a **Branch** node right after the sprint function trigger. Find the **InputAction Sprint** node and break its **Pressed** execution pin connection with the **Set Max Walk Speed** node. Add and connect a **Branch** node to the **Pressed** execution pin. Its output execution pin should then be connected to the **Set Max Walk Speed** node to again establish a complete chain. Now that the branch node is set up, we need to establish the condition that will allow the left shift trigger to continue activating the speed change through the **True** branch.

Drag the **Condition** input pin of the **Branch** node onto empty grid space and add a **Float >= Float** node. Drag the variables **Player Stamina** and **Sprint Costs** onto the grid, selecting the **Get** node for both. Attach **Get Player Stamina** to the top input pin of the **Float >= Float** node and attach **Get Sprint Cost** to the bottom input. The final result should look like the following screenshot:

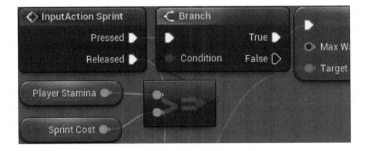

Regenerating stamina

The final element of stamina and sprinting we'll create is background stamina regeneration, so that the player has a way of recovering from running out of stamina. To accomplish this, we'll be taking advantage of the **Event Tick** trigger to increment the player's stamina gradually:

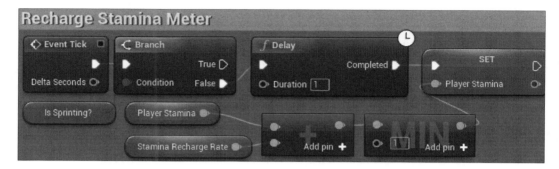

To create the event shown in the preceding screenshot, start by finding some empty grid space and add an **Event Tick** node. Attach a **Branch** node to the **Event Tick** node's output execution pin. Drag the variable **Is Sprinting?** onto the **Condition** pin to create a **Get Is Sprinting?** node attached the **Branch** node.

As **Event Tick** fires each frame, we want to force this function to wait until a regular amount of time in seconds has passed. To do this, we'll be using a **Delay** node. Drag a wire from the **False** output execution pin of the **Branch** node and attach it to a **Delay** node. Set the **Duration** field to 1 to ensure that the stamina recharge only happens once per second.

Next, drag out the **Player Stamina** variable, create a **Set** node, and attach it to the **Completed** output execution pin of the **Delay** node. Drag a wire from the input pin of this node out to empty grid space and add a **Min (Float)** node. This node will output the lowest value float that is linked among its inputs. As our stamina meter has a scale from 0 to 1, and we want to ensure it never goes over 1, type in 1 into the bottom input field.

Now drag a wire from the top input pin and attach it to a **Float + Float** node. Attach a **Get Player Stamina** node to the top input pin of this addition node. For the bottom pin, we'll want to determine a recharge rate. Create a new variable inside the **My Blueprint** panel and call it **StaminaRechargeRate**. Set its type to **Float**, check the checkbox labeled **Editable**, and set its default value to 0.05. Finally, drag that variable out and attach a **Get Stamina Recharge Rate** node to the bottom input pin of the **Float + Float** node.

Compile, save, and play to test our work. You'll now see that running out of stamina will block subsequent uses of sprint until additional stamina has been restored through the recharging effect.

Preventing firing actions when out of ammo

For the next constraint that we'll place on player abilities, we need to restrict the player from firing their gun when they reach an ammo count of **0**. To do so, find the group of nodes that manages firing the gun, grouped by the comment block labeled **Spawn projectile**. We will add a branch statement right after the **InputAction Fire** trigger that starts this chain of nodes:

Start by breaking the connection between the **InputAction Fire** and **Montage Play** nodes, and then add and connect a **Branch** node between them. Now find the variable **PlayerCurrentAmmo** from the **My Blueprints** panel and drag it near the **Branch** node, selecting the **Get** option to place the **Get Player Current Ammo** node. Drag a wire from the output pin of this node and add an **Integer > Integer** node. Leave the bottom input field at its default value of **0**. Connect the output pin of the node to the input **Condition** pin of the **Branch** node.

Now compile, save, and test your game. You should find that the gun no longer fires when the ammo counter reaches **0**.

Creating collectable objects

Restricting the player from firing their gun when they run out of ammo forces the player to be considerate of the accuracy of the shots they attempt within the game. However, limiting ammo would be unduly punishing without a way of acquiring more. We don't want ammo to naturally recharge like our stamina meter. Instead, we'll create a collectable item to allow the player to regain ammo by exploring and traversing the level.

Setting up collection logic

To create a collectable item, we will first want to start a new Blueprint that will determine the properties of each instance of that object that appears in the world. To do so, navigate to the **Content Browser** of the editor and open the `Blueprints` folder. Add a new **Blueprint** class, choose the class type **Actor**, and name it **AmmoPickup**. Once the Blueprint is made, double click on **AmmoPickup** to open the Blueprint editor.

In the viewport window that appears, we will see a simple white sphere. This is the default appearance given to empty actor objects before a mesh has been applied. To give the object a visible shape in the game, we first need to add a **Static Mesh** component to the Blueprint. Find the **Components** panel, click **Add Component**, and choose the **Static Mesh** option.

In the **Details** panel that appears, find the **Static Mesh** category with the field currently hosting the word **None** as no static mesh has yet been attached. In addition to attaching the **Static Mesh** component to the Blueprint giving the ability for a mesh to be associated with this Blueprint, we also need to designate which mesh will be displayed for that **Static Mesh** component.

Click on the drop-down menu for the static mesh, and then click on the bottom right button labeled **View Options**. In the popup menu that appears, ensure both **Show Plugin Content** and **Show Engine Content** have checked checkboxes next to them. This ensures that the assets included from plugins you installed in the engine and the default assets Epic included in the engine are seen in asset search results:

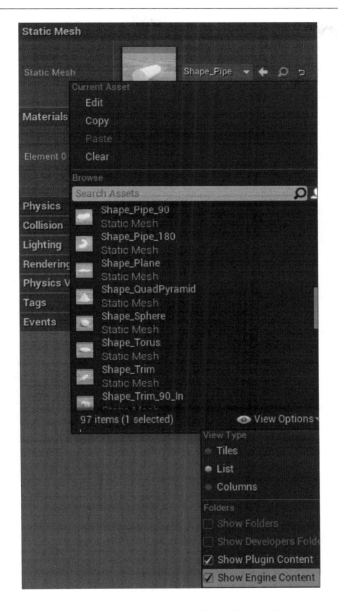

With the drop-down menu now properly searching for engine assets, search for **Shape_Pipe** and choose it. This mesh was not made for ammo pickups explicitly, but this item will be small enough that we can make it serve our purpose. Right below the **Static Mesh** category, find the **Materials** field and attach the material called **M_Door**. Finally, edit the **Transform** category's **Scale** values to be half their default size, 0.5 across the *x*, *y*, and *z* axes.

While design prototyping a game, it is most often useful to take advantage of readily available assets rather than taking the time to create each asset from scratch. This allows you to focus your time and effort on determining what mechanics will result in the best play experience rather than spending time creating art assets that might later be discarded if the mechanic is removed from the design.

After adding the mesh, we need to add a collider of some kind so that other objects, such as the player character, can physically interact with our pickup. In the **Components** panel, with the **StaticMesh** component already selected, click on **Add Component** and add a **Capsule Collision** component. A thin orange line will appear in the viewport panel, representing the boundaries of the capsule shape collision. Minor adjustments to the position, rotation, and scale of the collision will be necessary in order to ensure that the entire mesh is contained inside of the collision that should surround it. This can be done using the transform controls at the top of the viewport panel or by using the shortcut keys *w* (for moving), *e* (for rotating), and *r* (for scaling).

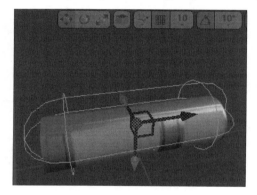

With the mesh and collider added, click on the **Event Graph** tab to begin adding Blueprint logic to our collectable. In the **Event Graph** tab, start by adding the trigger **Event Actor Begin Overlap**. This trigger will activate subsequent Blueprint nodes when the object attached to this Blueprint collides with any other object. In this case, we want our ammo collectable to be picked up when the player walks into the object:

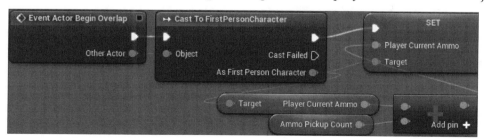

To ensure that the ammo collectable only activates when the player walks over it and that collecting an ammo pickup can impact the player's ammo counter, we first need to ensure that we are casting as the player. Attach a **Cast To FirstPersonCharacter** node to the **Event Actor Begin Overlap** trigger. Finally, connect the **Other Actor** output pin to the input **Object** pin of the casting node.

Now, we have a triggered event happening when the player character moves over our collectable object. When this happens, we want to add ammo to the player's ammo count. To do so, drag out a wire from **As First Person Character** output pin and attach it to a new **Set Player Current Ammo** node. Next, drag a second wire from **As First Person Character** output pin and attach it to a **Get Player Current Ammo** node. Drag the output pin from this new node and attach it to an **Int + Int** node. Next, drag the output pin from the **Int + Int** node back to the **Player Current Ammo** input pin of **Set Player Current Ammo** node.

The final step is to determine how much ammo to add when ammo collectables are picked up. To allow this number to be flexible, let's create a new editable variable called **Ammo Pickup Count**. Add this variable from the **My Blueprints** panel setting it to an **Int** type variable. Ensure that the **Editable** checkbox is checked, compile the Blueprint, and then set the variable's default value to 15. Finally, drag a **Get Ammo Pickup Count** node and attach it to the bottom input pin of the **Int + Int** node.

Next, let's trigger a sound and destroy the object itself when the collectable is picked up, as shown in the following diagram:

Drag a **Play Sound at Location** node and connect it to the output pin of the **Set Player Current Ammo**. Using only sounds provided in the engine, I found the **CompileSuccess** sound wave to work for our needs, so ensure that the **View Engine Content** is checked under **View Options**, and then select that file from the **Sound** drop-down menu.

We want to trigger that sound at the location of the ammo pickup, so attach a **Get Actor Location** node to the **Location** pin of the **Sound** node. Finally, add a **Destroy Actor** node at the end of the chain to ensure that each collectable can only be grabbed once. Compile and save the Blueprint.

Now return to the level, and drag the **AmmoPickup** Blueprint into the level. Do this two or three times in different locations around the level to seed the area with ammo pickups. When you are satisfied, save and click **Play** to test the game. You should see your ammo counter increase every time you step onto one of the ammo pickups.

Setting a gameplay win condition

One of the final steps we need to establish a full game loop is to create a condition for the player to win. To do so, we will modify our HUD and controller Blueprints to account for a target goal that the player must strive to hit.

Displaying a target goal in the HUD

First, we need to create a variable that will establish how many targets we are asking the player to destroy in order to achieve a win. Open up the FirstPersonCharacter Blueprint and create a new variable called TargetGoal. Make it an **Integer** variable type, ensure **Editable** is checked, and then set its default value to 2 for now.

Now that we have created a target goal, we should display this information to the player. Open the HUD Blueprint widget we created under our UI folder. From the **Designer** view, find the **Hierarchy** panel. Drag two more **Text** objects from the **Palette** panel onto the **Goal Tracker** object in the **Hierarchy**. For the first text object, change the **Text** field to / , *including the space before and after the slash*. For the second text object, find the **Text** field and enter 0. You might have to adjust the size of **Goal Tracker** object and click the button next to it to create a new binding.

Now, looking at the **Graph** view, select the new function Get_TargetGoal_Text_0. Similar to the other HUD bindings we created in the last chapter, we'll need to take the target goal variable from the **FirstPersonCharacter** Blueprint and return that value in this function, as shown in the following screenshot:

Create a **Get Player Character** node and drag its output pin onto a **Cast To FirstPersonCharacter** node. Drag a wire from the casting node's **As First Person Character** output pin and attach it to a **Get Target Goal** node. Next, drag the **Target Goal** output pin onto the **Return Value** input pin of the **ReturnNode**. Finally, connect the casting node to **Get Target Goal Text 0** on the input execution pin and **ReturnNode** on the output.

Compile, save, and play the game. You should see that the target counter increments upward as targets are destroyed. The displayed goal number shown to its right does not change. Now, we need to ensure that the player gets feedback when they reach their target goal.

Creating a win menu screen

To give the player feedback once they have won our game, we are going to create a win menu screen that will appear upon destroying the requisite number of targets. To create a menu, we are going to need another Blueprint widget, like what we developed for the HUD. Navigate to the **UI** folder we created and add a new **Blueprint Widget** found under **User Interface** in the add menu. Name this Blueprint WinMenu.

We are going to set up three elements for this menu screen. The first will be a simple text object that broadcasts to the player **You Win!**. The other two elements will be buttons that allow the player to restart the game or quit out of it. To start with, drag in two **Button** objects and one **Text** object onto the **CanvasPanel**. Next, select the **Text** object and change its **Text** field to say **You Win!**. Change the font size to 72 and the font color to a light green, and then resize and reposition the text object on the canvas so that it appears in the top middle of the screen, but a little lower than you placed your HUD objects in the previous chapter. Finally, anchor the object to the top middle of the screen by selecting the second option from the **Anchors** selector.

Now, drag an additional **Text** object, and place one on top of both **Button** objects. Rename the two **Button** objects **Restart** button and **Quit** button. Change the size of the buttons so that they are roughly the same size as our **You Win!** textbox and stack them below the text display. Anchor both buttons to the center of the screen.

Next, select the **Text** object under the **Restart** button and change its **Text** field to **Restart**. Then, change the font size to 60. Change font color to black to ensure it shows up on our gray buttons. Finally, click on the second button for both the **Horizontal Alignment** and **Vertical Alignment** settings. Do the same operations on the **Text** object attached to the **Quit** button, except that the **Text** field should display the text **Quit**.

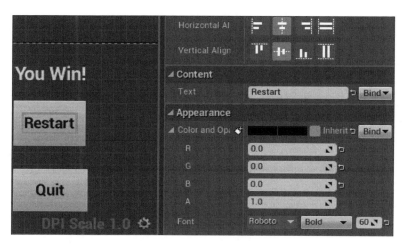

Now we need to add actions that will fire when the buttons are pressed. Click on the **Restart** button object, scroll down to the bottom of the **Details** panel, and click on the + button next to the **OnClicked** event. This will add an event that triggers when the button is clicked.

You will be taken to the graph view, where a **OnClicked (Restart** button) node will appear. Attach an **Open Level** node to this. Type in the name of your level into the **Level Name** field, ensuring accuracy of spelling. If you've been following along and have not changed the name of the level from the template, this will be **FirstPersonExampleMap**. Doing this will reopen the level when the player clicks on the button, resetting all aspects of the level, including targets, ammo collectables, and the player.

After the **Open Level** node, attach a **Remove from Parent** node. This node tells our WinMenu objects to stop displaying. We want the menu to go away once the level is reset.

Now return to the designer view and click on the **Quit** button object. Click on the + button next to the **OnClicked** event here as well. You'll be taken back to the graph view, this time with a new **OnClicked (Quit** button) node. Attach a **Quit Game** node to this event so that the player can shut down the game by clicking the **Quit** button, as shown here:

Displaying the menu

Now that our menu has been created, we need to tell the game when to show it to the player. As we called our HUD objects from within the `FirstPersonCharacter` Blueprint, let's go ahead and call this menu from the same location. Open `FirstPersonCharacter` in the `Blueprints` folder.

We are going to need to trigger off some event that will signal the end of the game. Before we even determine what that signal will be, we can create a **Custom Event** node to represent it. Add a **Custom Event** node to some empty graph space and rename it to **End Game**.

When the victory condition is met, we want to stop the player from continuing to move around the game world. To do so, attach a **Set Game Paused** node to our event and check the **Paused** checkbox. Next, add a **Get Player Controller** node below the **End Game** event node. Drag out its **Return Value** output pin and attach it to a **Set Show Mouse Cursor** node. Check the checkbox next to **Show Mouse Cursor** and attach this node to the output execution pin of **Set Game Paused**. This will enable the player to regain control over the mouse cursor after the game is paused, as shown here:

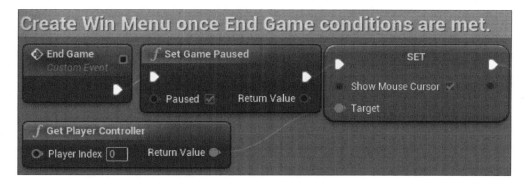

Now that we have stopped the game from playing, we want to actually display the menu. Attach a **Create Widget** node to the end of the chain and select **Win Menu** from the **Class** dropdown. To conclude this Blueprint chain, drag a wire from the **Return Value** output pin and attach it to an **Add to Viewport** node.

Triggering a win

The final step for us is to determine the conditions that will result in the **End Game** custom event being triggered. We want the event to happen once the player has killed a sufficient number of target cylinders to meet the target goal. We can evaluate this each time a target is destroyed. To do so, open **CylinderTarget_Blueprint** in the `Blueprints` folder and navigate to the end of the Blueprint chain in the event graph.

We want to create a **Branch** node that will allow us to check if the last destroyed target was the last one needed to reach the goal. Attach a **Branch** node to the **Set Target Kill Count** node near the end of the chain. You can reattach the **Destroy Actor** node to the **False** output of the **Branch** node.

Now we need to establish the condition that the branch will check. We are going to want to compare the **Target Kill Count** variable to see if it has reached or exceeded the **Target Goal** variable. To do so, create an **Int >= Int** node and drag its output pin to the **Condition** pin of the **Branch** node.

Next, find the **Get Target Kill Count** node that already exists and drag a second wire from its output pin to the top input pin of the **Int >= Int** node. Then, find the **Cast to FirstPersonCharacter** node and drag out a wire from its **As First Person Character** output pin onto a new **Get Target Goal** node. Drag the output pin of this new node to the bottom input pin of the **Int >= Int** node.

Now drag a third wire from the **Cast to FirstPersonCharacter** node's output pin and attach it to a new **End Game** node, which will call our custom event. Connect this node to the **True** output of the **Branch** node, and then make a second connection to the **Destroy Actor** node after it. This should complete your branching logic and produce a result that looks like the following screenshot:

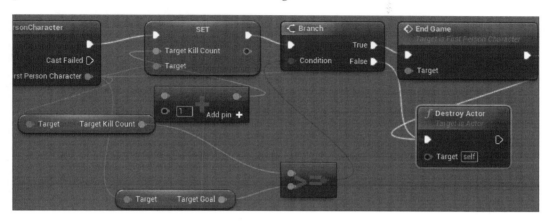

Compile, save, and press play to test the game. If all of the Blueprints are set up correctly, you should see the game pause and a victory menu appear as soon as you destroy a second target. Clicking on the **Restart** button will reload the level from the start, and clicking **Quit** will close the play session.

Summary

In this chapter, we enhanced the play experience by providing productive constraints on the player's abilities and established a goal for the player to accomplish. In the process, you learned how to use timers to repeat actions, how to create collectable objects in the game world, and how to create a menu system. The components that make up the foundation of a video game experience are all present in the game that we've built. If you desire, you could spend some time customizing the level layout to create a properly challenging game experience that is uniquely yours.

In the next chapter, we'll begin tackling a more advanced subject of Blueprint scripting and game development—artificial intelligence. We will replace our target cylinders with enemies that can patrol between points and pursue the player around the level.

5
Making Moving Enemies with AI

In this chapter, we'll be adding additional challenge to our gameplay by making enemies that pose a threat to the player. To do so, we'll leave behind our target cylinders in favor of enemies that have AI behavior. We want to set up enemies that have the potential to pose a threat to the player and are capable of analyzing the world around them in order to make decisions. To accomplish this, you are going to learn about Unreal Engine 4's built-in tools for handling AI behavior and how those tools interact with our Blueprint scripting. In this process, we will accomplish the following goals:

- Constructing an AI that is capable of decision-making using a Behavior Tree, a Blackboard, and an AI Controller
- Creating a patrol path in the level that the AI will follow using a NavMesh
- Modifying the AI to pursue the player character when they see the player

Setting up the enemy actor to navigate

Until now, our targets have been represented by basic cylinder geometry. This worked well for prototyping a non-responsive target that is present only as an aiming challenge for the player. However, an enemy that will move around and present a threat to the player will need a recognizable appearance that will at least broadcast to the player its direction of travel. Fortunately for us, Epic has created a freely available asset package with Unreal Engine 4, which we can use to bring in a humanoid model into our game — one that is perfect for our new enemy type.

Importing from the marketplace

For this step, we'll step out of the Unreal Engine editor and will focus on the Epic Games Launcher. Open the launcher and navigate to the **Marketplace** section along the left-hand side of the window. The asset we are interested in is in the **Characters** and **Animations** section of the **Marketplace**. Once you're there, find the **Animation Starter Pack**, which should have a noticeable green **FREE** banner over the image of a blue character. Click on this image and you will be taken to the asset page.

Next, click on the green **Free** button. After a moment, the button should turn into a yellow **Download** button. Click on this button and wait as the asset package is downloaded to your computer. Once this is done, the button will be replaced once more with a yellow **Add to project** button. Click on this button and select the project you have been using to build your game. A folder called AnimStarterPack will be added to the Content folder of your project.

Expanding the play area

In order to provide an interesting environment for our intelligent enemies to chase the player, we might need to make some changes in the default first person example map layout. The existing layout, while being serviceable for target shooting, is likely too cramped for a player to be able to successfully avoid an enemy that is chasing them.

Level design does not directly intersect with Blueprint scripting, so we won't go through a step-by-step process of how you should modify your level. Instead, we'll take this chance to customize the experience to the kind of game experience you would like to provide. Minimally, you'll want to modify the layout of the map so that there is additional space to move around. You might also create some areas for the player to be able to take cover or areas that would make for interesting patrol points for enemies. Basic manipulation of the level can be accomplished by moving existing objects around in the 3D Viewport. You can expand the size of the play space by moving the walls that make up the boundaries. You can also add additional basic objects, such as cubes and spheres, to your level to serve as additional obstacles or cover.

To quickly give a little bit of additional variety to the gameplay, I chose to create a second level accessible by ramp to both the player and enemies. I also expanded the play area to be twice as wide as it was earlier. An image of the quick layout modifications I made is shown in the the following screenshot:

As you change the position of static objects in the level, you will see a prompt that *lighting needs to be rebuilt*. This is because lighting information is attached (or in engine terms, it's *baked*) to static objects ahead of time to increase performance once the game is played. After you are done with your changes to the level, click on the **Build** button to rebuild the lighting information with your new object layout.

Also note that when changing the physical dimensions and placement of the walls that surround the template map, you will also want to increase the size of the `LightmassImportanceVolume`. This will ensure that your entire playable area gets the same high-quality lighting treatment.

Making the level traversable with a NavMesh

In order to create AI behavior that allows our enemies to traverse the level, we need to create a map of the environment that the AI will know how to read and navigate with. This map is created with an object known as a **NavMesh**. To create a NavMesh, find the **Modes** panel. With the **Place** tab selected, click on **Volumes** and then drag the **Nav Mesh Bounds Volume** object out onto the level.

Now you will want to move and scale up the **Nav Mesh Bounds Volume** until the entire walkable space of your level is contained within it. When you think you have your walking areas contained within the volume, press the *P* key on your keyboard to see if the NavMesh is placed correctly. If so, you'll see a green mesh on top of your floors, as seen in the following screenshot:

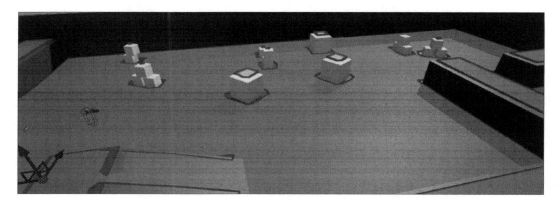

 You can press *P* at any time to toggle the green NavMesh visibility on and off.

Setting the stage for intelligence with AI assets

With our level and NavMesh now set up, we can return our focus to creating the enemy. First, we need to establish a Blueprint that will contain the enemy character. From your project directory in the **Content Browser**, create a new folder called `Enemy`. Open this folder; right-click on empty space and select **Blueprint Class**. Open the **All Classes** group at the bottom of the popup and type `ASP` into the search bar. Select the `ASP_Character` object to create a new character Blueprint. We'll name this Blueprint as `EnemyCharacter`.

Now that we have a Blueprint to contain our enemy character, we need to create three additional objects that will work together to manage the behavior of our enemy. The first of these is called a **Behavior Tree**. A Behavior Tree is the source of the decision-making logic that will instruct our enemy on what conditions should cause it to perform which actions. To create a Behavior Tree, right-click in the folder and then on the **Miscellaneous** category; now, select **Behavior Tree**. Name the new Behavior Tree as `EnemyBehavior`.

The second object we need to create is an **AI Controller**. The AI Controller will serve as a connection between the character and the Behavior Tree. It routes the information and actions that are generated within the Behavior Tree to the character, which will enact those actions. To create an AI Controller, right-click in the folder and click on **Blueprint Class**; now search for and select **AIController**. Name this controller EnemyController.

The final object we'll create to control the behavior is called a **Blackboard**. A Blackboard is a container for all of the data that an AI controller needs to be governed by its Behavior Tree. To create a Blackboard, right-click in the folder and click on the **Miscellaneous** category; now select **Blackboard**. Predictably, we'll name this Blackboard EnemyBlackboard.

Next, we should make some modifications to EnemyCharacter. Because we created EnemyCharacter as an ASP_Character object type, it inherited information about the desired mesh, texture, and animations from the character created for the animation pack we imported. Some of this information, such as the mesh and support for the animations, we will want to keep. However, we need to ensure that it knows how to be controlled by the right AI Controller. To change this, open the EnemyCharacter Blueprint now.

With EnemyCharacter open, look at the **Components** panel. Click on **EnemyCharacter(self)**, which will be the top item in the components list. Now look at the **Details** panel and find the **Pawn** category. The last element of this category will be a drop-down list for the AI Controller Class. Change the selection of this drop-down list to our new EnemyController.

While we're editing EnemyCharacter, we should change the color of the enemy as well. Currently, the mesh shows a blue humanoid that appears to be of the same style as that of the player's arms and gun. To better indicate to the player that the character is an enemy, we can change the mesh to use the same TargetRed material we used for the cylinders in the previous chapters. To do so, click on **Mesh (Inherited)** and find the **Materials** category in the **Details** panel. Change the material from the blue default to the **TargetRed** material we created. You should see the humanoid character in the viewport change into a red color. Compile and save it and return to the level editor. Drag the **EnemyCharacter** Blueprint onto the level to create an instance of an enemy in our map. Rename the instance of **EnemyCharacter** in the **World Outliner** to Enemy1.

Creating navigation behavior

The first goal for our enemy will be to get it to navigate between points we create on the map. To accomplish this, we'll need to create points on the map that the enemy will be navigating to, and then we need to set up the behavior that will cause the enemy to move to each of the points in a cycle.

Setting up patrol points

Let's start by creating the path we want the AI to patrol. While still being in the level editor, look at the **Modes** panel. With the **Place** tab selected, click on **All Classes** and drag a **Target Point** object onto the area of the map that you would like for the enemy to start the patrol. Now look at the **World Outliner** panel and click on the folder icon with a plus symbol that sits to the right of the search bar. Click on this to create a new folder called `PatrolPoints`. This folder will contain all of the points we create so that we can keep the main list tidy. Drag the **TargetPoint** object in the outliner into this new folder and rename the object as `PatrolPoint1`.

Now go to the **Details** panel of `PatrolPoint1` and click on the green **Add Component** button. Add a **Sphere Collider** to the patrol point. Adding a collider will allow us to check whenever the enemy actor overlaps with the patrol point.

Duplicate the **PatrolPoint1** object in the **World Outliner** by right-clicking on it and clicking on **Edit** and then on **Duplicate**. The new object will automatically be named as `PatrolPoint2`. Drag the second patrol point somewhere else in the level, far enough away from the first so that movement between the two points would be noticeable:

The **target point** is a small crosshair icon that will appear only in edit mode for the level but is invisible to the player while the game is running. This allows us to visualize the route we are creating for the enemy without having a visual artifact in play mode that looks distracting or gives information away.

Enabling communication between assets

With our patrol points established, we can transition to building the intelligence of our enemy. To begin, we are going to give our Blackboard the ability to store information about the location of a patrol point. Open **EnemyBlackboard** from the **Content Browser**. Click on **New Key** and select **Object** as the **Key Type**. Call this new object key as `PatrolPoint`, as shown in the following screenshot.

Now that we have a `Patrol Point` key setup within our Blackboard, we need to set the value of that key within the Blackboard to the actual patrol point object in the world. We can do this from the `EnemyCharacter` Blueprint, so open the character Blueprint now.

We want to create a sequence that starts when the enemy character is created and then grabs the `EnemyBlackboard`. It will then set the key value called `Patrol Point` inside the Blackboard to the value contained within a variable we will create for the character Blueprint representing the enemy's current patrol point target, as shown in the following screenshot:

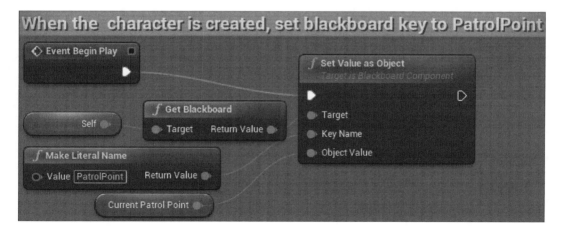

First, we want to create a variable that will store our two patrol point objects. Add a new variable from the **My Blueprint** panel and call it PatrolPoint1. Set the **Variable Type** to **Actor**. Now right-click on the variable, and duplicate it. Call this duplicate PatrolPoint2. Finally, duplicate the Actor variable a third time and call this variable CurrentPatrolPoint. We will change the patrol point stored in this variable each time we want to move the enemy to a new location.

With the three variables created, we next want to create an **Event Begin Play** node. Next, add a **Get Blackboard** node. Drag a wire from the **Target** input pin; search for and select **Get Reference to Self** to attach a **Self** node to the pin. Now drag a wire from the **Return Value** pin and attach it to a **Set Value as Object** node. Connect this node's input execution pin to the **Event Begin Play** node.

Returning to the **Set Value as Object** node, drag a wire from the **Key Name** input and attach it to a **Make Literal Name** node. Set the **Value** field within this node to PatrolPoint so that it references the key we created inside the Blackboard. Finally, drag the Patrol Point variable to the **Event Graph**, and select **Get**. Connect the **Get Patrol Point** node to the **Object Value** input pin of **Set Value as Object**. Select all of these nodes and create a comment for yourself that describes the functionality.

Next, we want to create a series of nodes that will swap the patrol point the enemy is moving toward each time they successfully reach one of their two patrol points. To do this, we will create two branches that will trigger off a detection of a collider overlap, as shown in the following screenshot:

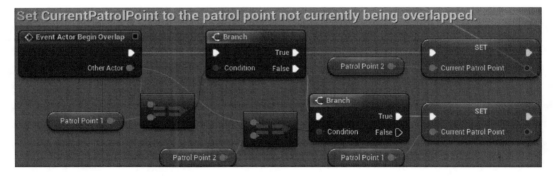

Begin by creating an **Event Actor Begin Overlap** node. Attach this node to a **Branch** node. Drag a wire from the **Condition** input of the **Branch** node onto an **Equal** (Object) node. This node evaluates whether the two objects attached to the two inputs of the node are identical to one another. In our case, we want to evaluate whether the object being overlapped by the enemy is the same object that is attached to the **Patrol Point 1** variable.

Drag a wire from the **Other Actor** output pin of **Event Actor Begin Overlap** node and attach it to the top input pin of the **Equal** (Object) node. Now drag the **Patrol Point 1** variable onto the graph and attach a **Get Patrol Point 1** node to the bottom input pin of the **Equal** (Object) node. If these two objects are equal, we want to change the **Current Patrol Point** variable to **Patrol Point 2**. From the **True** output pin of the **Branch** node, attach a wire to a **Set Current Patrol Point** node and attach a **Get Patrol Point 2** node to its input pin.

Next, we need to create a second branch series to test against the other patrol point. Drag a wire from the **False** output pin of the **Branch** node and attach it to a second **Branch** node. Attach the **Condition** input pin of this new **Branch** node to a new **Equal** (Object) node. Connect the top input pin of the **Equal** (Object) node to the **Other Actor** output pin of **Event Actor Begin Overlap** node.

Drag the second patrol point variable onto the graph and attach a **Get Patrol Point 2** node to the bottom input pin of **Equal** (Object). Now attach the **True** output pin of the second **Branch** node to a new **Set Current Patrol Point** node. Then, attach a **Get Patrol Point 1** node to the input pin of **Set Current Patrol Point**. Finally, attach the output execution pins of both **Set Control Patrol Point** nodes to the input execution pin of the **Set Value as Object** node in the other block of Blueprint nodes we used to set the Blackboard key. This final step is important to ensure that the updated **Current Patrol Point** value gets sent to the Blackboard every time the variable changes value.

This finishes the work we have inside **EnemyCharacter**. Next, we need to go to the AI Controller and instruct it to run the Behavior Tree that we'll be setting up. Return to the **Content Browser** and open **EnemyController**.

In the **Event Graph** of **EnemyController**, add an **Event Begin Play** node. Connect this node to a **Run Behavior Tree** node. Finally, set the **BTAsset** inside this node to **EnemyBehavior**. That's all there is to do with the controller, as shown in the following screenshot:

Return now to the level editor and select the **Enemy1** object in the **World Outliner** panel. Recall that this was the name we gave to the first instance of the generic enemy type we're creating. We want to establish the initial patrol point for this particular enemy. To do so, look at the **Details** panel and find the **Patrol Point** field under **Default**; now select the object **PatrolPoint1** in the drop-down list.

Teaching our AI to walk with the Behavior Tree

We can now move on to the heart of the AI—the Behavior Tree. Return to the **Content Browser** and open **EnemyBehavior**. On the right, change the **Blackboard Asset** to **EnemyBlackboard**. You should now see our Blackboard key **PatrolPoint** appear in the **Blackboard** panel on the bottom left.

Now look at the **Behavior Tree** panel, which will look similar to the event graphs we are used to seeing inside of Blueprints. This is where we'll create the branching logic that will determine which actions to perform, based on the conditions it is currently experiencing. The top level of the logic tree will always be the **Root**, which simply serves to indicate where the logic flow will start.

The darker line at the bottom of the Behavior Tree nodes is the connection point between nodes. You can click and drag a wire from the dark area at the bottom of the **Root** node and drop it onto empty space to get a new selection menu popup that will allow you to add additional nodes to the Behavior Tree. Do so now and select the **Selector** option, as shown in the following screenshot:

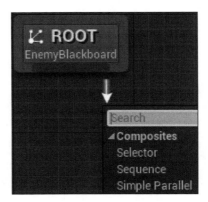

The two primary branching node types you'll utilize are the **Selector** and the **Sequence**. A Selector node runs each of the nodes connected underneath it, called its **children**, left to right but succeeds and stops running as soon as one child successfully runs. Thus, if a Selector has three children, the only way the third child node will be run is if the first two children failed to execute because the conditions attached to them were false. A Sequence node is just the opposite. It runs all of the children in sequence left to right also, but the Sequence node only succeeds if all of the children succeed. The first child to fail causes the whole Sequence to fail, ending the execution and aborting the Sequence.

Underneath the **Selector** node, attach two **Sequence** nodes next to one another. Select the **Sequence** node on the left and change the **Node Name** in the **Description** panel to `Move to Patrol`. Next, select the other **Sequence** node and change its name to `Idle`.

 Notice the faint grey circles with numbers inside of them that are positioned to the upper right corner of the two **Sequence** nodes. These indicate the execution order of the nodes, which are ordered according to their left to right positions. The first node to be evaluated will be labeled with a **0** badge.

Now we need to add actions that will be triggered by the **Sequence** nodes. Drag a wire down from the **Move to Patrol** node and attach a **Move To** node. This node will be purple in color, visually distinguished as a node that results in actions. These nodes are called **task nodes** and will always be the bottommost nodes in a Behavior Tree. As a consequence, you will notice there is no attachment point for additional nodes at the bottom of a task node, as shown in the following screenshot:

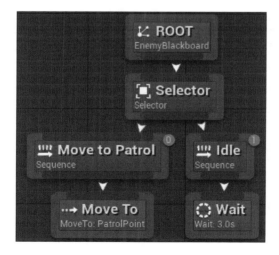

Looking at the **Details** panel of our newly added **Move To** task node, you will notice a few new options that are available for us to tweak the movement of our enemy character. The first of these is a field called **Acceptable Radius**. This field indicates the number of units the actor being controlled by the move task can be away from the target before the task is considered complete. Setting the **Acceptable Radius** too low might cause the enemy to appear jerky as it tries to move to the exact center of the patrol point. Setting it too high might result in the movement being cut too short, as the move is considered complete long before the enemy touches the patrol point. Set the **Acceptable Radius** to 30 for a safe middle ground that matches the default radius of a sphere collider and will have the AI stopping at a proximity to the target that looks good. We don't want the enemy to move sideways or strafe toward the target, so we can leave **Allow Strafe** unchecked. The **Blackboard Key** determines the location that the actor will be moved to. As we only have one Blackboard Key, it should be automatically set to our intended target which is **PatrolPoint**.

Next, drag a wire down from the node that we called **Idle** and attach it to a **Wait** task node. The **Wait** node contains only two configuration fields. The **Wait Time** field value determines how long the enemy will wait between movements to the next patrol point. Set this value to 3.0 to add a three second pause between patrols. The field below, named **Random Deviation**, allows us to add randomness to the amount of time that passes while waiting. Enter 1.0 into this field to add a one second variation to our three second wait time. This will result in a pause of random length between two and four seconds between patrols.

Compile and save the Behavior Tree and then return to the **FirstPersonExampleMap** tab. Find the enemy we placed called **Enemy1** and select it in the **World Outliner**. In the **Details** panel, navigate down to the **Default** category and set **Patrol Point 1** to the object **PatrolPoint1**, **Patrol Point 2** to the object **PatrolPoint2**, and set **Current Patrol Point** to the patrol point object furthest away from the enemy's starting position. We want to set these patrol points on the enemy instance in the world rather than as defaults on the variables within the enemy Blueprint because we want each enemy that we create in the future to have its own set of patrol points, as shown in the following screenshot:

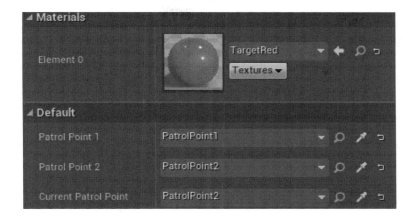

Save and click **Play** to test. You should see the red enemy character start navigating to the first of the two patrol points. When it reaches the first point, it will briefly pause and then start walking to the second patrol point. This pattern will continue back and forth as long as the game is running.

Making the AI chase the player

Now that we have a patrol behavior established, we should make the enemy pose some threat to the player. To do so, we will give the enemy the ability to see the player and pursue them.

Giving the enemy sight with Pawn Sensing

To grant the enemy the ability to detect the player, we need to add a `PawnSensing` component to the `EnemyController`. To do this, open the **EnemyController** Blueprint and click on the **Add Component** button in the **Components** panel. Search for and add the **PawnSensing** component. This component gives us the ability to add a few additional event triggers to the `EnemyController` event graph. The one we are interested in now is called **OnSeePawn (PawnSensing)**, as shown here:

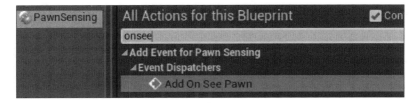

There is a second system that can be used for AI behavior development and environment sensing called the **Environment Query System (EQS)**. As of Unreal Engine version 4.7.6, this feature is still in the experimental development phase and has some bugs that prevent it from being recommended for current development. However, with the release of Unreal 4.8, the EQS features are expected to take over as the primary system for developing AI that can sense the environment around them. The pawn sensing behavior we cover in this book will remain usable alongside the new EQS system, and many of these concepts will transfer over. As with any new feature that gets introduced, the release of the feature will be paired with some basic documentation, which is available on Epic's website at `https://docs.unrealengine.com/latest/INT/`.

Ensure you have the new **PawnSensing** component selected in **Components** panel, and then with **Context Sensitive** searching checked, search for and add the **OnSeePawn** node to the event graph. This event fires when the enemy is able to see the player through line of sight. To transmit this information to our Behavior Tree, we will first need to create a new Blackboard Key store and pass this information to it. You can see how this is accomplished in the following screenshot:

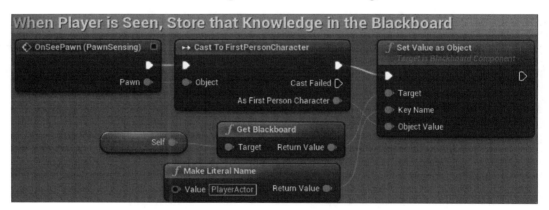

Drag a wire from the **Pawn** output pin of the **OnSeePawn** node we just created and attach it to a **Cast To FirstPersonCharacter** node. This will ensure that the enemy only reacts to the player being seen as we do not want to trigger a chase behavior when it sees other enemies.

Next, we need to get a reference to the Blackboard. Add a **Get Blackboard** node to the event graph. Drag a wire from the **Target** input pin of this node and attach a **Self** node to it. Now drag a wire from the **Return Value** output pin and attach it to a **Set Value as Object** node. Then, connect the **As First Person Character** output pin of the casting node to the **Object Value** input pin of the **Set Value as Object** node. Also, connect the execution pins of the **Cast to FirstPersonCharacter** and **Set Value as Object** nodes.

The final step to pass the information about the player being spotted to the Blackboard is to establish the key that will store the data. Drag a wire from the **Key Name** input pin of **Set Value as Object** and attach it to a **Make Literal Name** node. We don't yet have a key created on the Blackboard for this purpose, but that will be our next step. For now, Enter `PlayerActor` into the **Value** field of this node. As always, create a comment around the block of nodes reminding yourself of its functionality; then compile and save your work.

Adding conditions to the Behavior Tree

Now, we need to create our Blackboard Key and create the Behavior Tree branch that will instruct the enemy to chase the player. Open **EnemyBehavior** from the **Content Browser** and then click on the **Blackboard** tab. Click on the **New Key** button and create a new key of the **Object** type called `PlayerActor`. With the **PlayerActor** key selected, look at the **Blackboard Details** panel. Click on the expansion arrow next to **Key Type** and change the **Base Class** to **Actor** with the drop-down. For reference, fill in the **Entry Description** to indicate that this key will store the player character and leave **Instance Synced** unchecked, as shown in the following screenshot:

Now save and click on the **Behavior Tree** tab. We will need another **Sequence** node that will connect to tasks to get the enemy to chase the player. Drag a wire down from the **Selector** node and create a **Sequence** node to the left of our **Move to Patrol** sequence node. Because we want the enemy seeing and chasing the player to take higher priority over their patrol and idle behaviors, we want to ensure this sequence is the left-most branch underneath selector. Change this new node's name to `Attack Player`.

Next, we want to ensure that the tasks attached to `Attack Player` only trigger when the enemy actually sees the player. To do this, we'll be adding a **decorator** node. A decorator node attaches to the top of sequences and provides conditions that must be met before that sequence can be triggered. Right-click on the **Attack Player** node; hover over **Add Decorator** to expand the menu and select **Blackboard** to add a new decorator that triggers off a Blackboard key. You will see a new blue box appear directly above the **Attack Player** sequence. Click on this and look at the **Details** panel, as shown in the following screenshot:

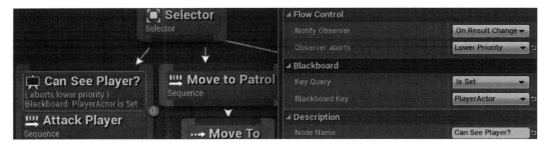

In the **Details** panel, find the **Observer aborts** dropdown and select the **Lower Priority** option. Combined with the **On Result Change** option that is selected by default for **Notify Observer**, this will indicate that when this condition changes to true, all of the other sequences that are of lower priority should be aborted. This will be visually indicated with a blue highlight around all of the lower priority sequence nodes in the Behavior Tree view when you have this decorator selected.

Next, ensure that the **Key Query** is set to **Is Set** and change the **Blackboard Key** to **PlayerActor**. This will check to ensure that the **PlayerActor** has a value set before it allows **Attack Player** to run. Recall that **PlayerActor** is only set when the enemy established line of sight with the player through its pawn sensing component. Finally, change the name of this node to **Can See Player?** to reflect its functionality.

Creating chasing behavior

Now, we need to create the series of task nodes underneath the **Attack Player** sequence that will make up the enemy's chasing behavior. Because we already have a Blackboard Key that stores the player actor, including its location data, moving the enemy character to the player is easy. Drag a wire from the **Attack Player** sequence node and attach it to a **Move To task** node. Click on this node, and in the **Details** panel, change the **Blackboard Key** to **PlayerActor**.

That's all that is necessary to get the enemy chasing the player! You can compile, save, and press play to test run this behavior. When you run in front of the enemy on its patrol path, it will break out of its path and begin pursuing you around the level. However, you will notice that no matter what you do, the enemy will never relent in its pursuit. As our end goal is to have the enemy reach the player and then return to its patrol, we'll need to create some way for the enemy to break out of the chase behavior.

To create a pause to allow an attack to happen, first create a **Wait** node and place it to the right of the **Move To** node. Change the **Wait Time** on this node to two seconds, which is roughly the time we might expect an attack to take. Combined with the **Move To**, this will cause the enemy to chase the player until they are in range and then wait two seconds before taking another action.

Now we need to create a way for the **PlayerActor** key to be reset so that the **Can See Player?** decorator can fail after the pause happens, thus ending the chase behavior. There is no built-in task to cover this functionality, so we'll need to create a custom task to handle this. Click on the **New Task** button along the top menu of the Behavior Tree, and select the **BTTask_BlueprintBase** option from the dropdown that appears. This creates a new task using the basic Blueprint class as its base class.

You'll be instantly taken to a new tab where you can begin editing the behavior of this task, but first let's return to the **Content Browser** to rename this task to something useful. Find the new task object called **BTTask_BlueprintBase_New** in the **Enemy** folder and rename the object to ResetValueTask. Double click on **ResetValueTask** to return to the task's tab.

Before adding any nodes, change the **Node Name** in the **Details** panel to Reset Value. Now go to the **My Blueprint** panel and add two variables. Call the first variable Key, and change its type to **BlackboardKeySelector**. Rename the second variable Actor, and change its type to **Actor**. Finally, ensure that both of the variables have the **Editable** checkbox checked, as shown in the following screenshot:

With our variables created and our nodes named, we can start creating the behavior of our task. Add an **Event Receive Execute** trigger node to the event graph. This node simply triggers the attached behaviors when the task is activated within the Behavior Tree. Next, drag a wire from the execution pin and attach a **Set Blackboard Value as Object** node. Drag the **Key** variable onto the **Key** input pin. Then drag the **Actor** variable to the **Value** input pin. Finally, drag a wire from the output execution pin of **Set Blackboard Value as Object** node and attach it to a **Finish Execute** node. Check the checkbox next to the **Success** input of this node. After giving the block of nodes a descriptive comment container, the final result should look like the following screenshot:

This task will allow us to designate a Blackboard Key from the **Details** panel of the task in the Behavior Tree and set that key to an actor of our choosing. We could have replaced the generic public variables we created with the specific values we want to set with this node, namely changing the **PlayerActor** key to null or empty. However, when making new tasks, it is a good practice to make them generically useful with reusable behavior that changes depending on the inputs given in the Behavior Tree. With the task made to fit our needs, compile the Blueprint, save, and return to the **EnemyBehavior** Behavior Tree.

Back in the Behavior Tree, drag a wire down from **Attack Player** and add our new **ResetValueTask** task node to the right of both the **Move To** and **Wait** nodes. In the **Details** panel, change the **Key** to **PlayerActor** and leave the **Actor** dropdown with a **None** value. Finally, change the **Node Name** to **Reset Player Seen**.

This completes our work in the Behavior Tree to establish chasing behavior. Compile, save, and press Play to test the behavior. As you navigate the player character in front of the patrolling enemy, the enemy will stop its patrol and chase the player. When the enemy reaches the player, it'll stop for two seconds before returning to its patrol path. If it re-establishes the line of sight with the player, it will interrupt its patrol and begin chasing the player again.

Summary

In this chapter, we began the process of changing our simple, moving targets into fleshed out game enemies that can challenge the player. In the process, you learned the fundamentals about how AI Controllers, Behavior Trees, and Blackboards can be leveraged together to create an enemy with the ability to sense the world around them and make decisions based on that information.

As we continue the process of developing our AI to pose a serious challenge to the player, you can use the skills you have learned to consider other kinds of behaviors you might be able to provide to an enemy. Continued exploration of AI mechanics will see you continually coming back to the core loop of sensing, decision making, and acting that we began implementing here.

In the next chapter, we'll be extending our AI behavior to create an enemy that can truly challenge the player. We will add the ability for the enemy to listen for the player and investigate a sound as well as give the enemy an attack ability to damage the player when they get too close. To balance the game around this new threat, we'll also give the player the ability to fight back against the enemies.

6
Upgrading the AI Enemies

In this chapter, we will be adding more functionality to our AI enemies to introduce the potential for the player to fail, and for greater gameplay diversity. At this point, we are going to begin settling on the kind of challenge we want to offer the player. We are going to create zombie-like enemies that will relentlessly pursue the player, creating an action-focused experience, where the player must try to survive against hoards of enemies. We will start by giving greater capability to the AI, including damage dealing and wandering patterns, in order to increase the difficulty of surviving. We will then turn our attention to the player, giving them the ability to fight back against these dangerous enemies. Finally, we will complete our difficulty balancing by creating a system to spawn new enemies in the game world over time. In the process, we will cover the following topics:

- Introducing an enemy melee attack that will damage the player's health
- Giving the AI the ability to hear the player's footsteps and shots
- Having the enemy investigate the last known location of the player based on sound
- Allowing the player to destroy the enemies with their gun
- Spawning new enemies in the world
- Setting AI enemies to wander the level randomly

Creating an enemy attack

If the enemies we create are going to pose a real obstacle that stand in the way of the player achieving the goals we create for them, we will first need to give the enemies the ability to damage the player. In the previous chapter, we set up the basic structure of an enemy attack pattern. It is triggered when the player enters the enemy's line of sight. We are now going to introduce a damage component to this attack, ensuring that there is some consequence of the enemy reaching melee range of the player.

Making an attack task

To create an attack task that does damage, we will be extending the `Attack Player` sequence we created in the enemy Behavior Tree. Open **EnemyBehavior** from **Content Browser** now. From the **Behavior Tree** view, click on the **New Task** button and select the **BTTask_BlueprintBase** option from the drop-down menu that appears. As we did with the custom task to reset key values in the previous chapter, we will want to navigate to the **Enemy** folder in **Content Browser**, and rename the newly created **BTTask_BlueprintBase_New** object to `DoAttackTask`. Double-click on **DoAttackTask** to return to **EventGraph** for the new task.

We will need to create two variables within the task, one to store the target of the damage, and one to store the amount of damage to be applied. From the **My Blueprint** panel, use the + sign button next to **Variables** to create two variables. Call the first variable `TargetActor`, set its type to **Blackboard Key**, and check the box next to **Editable** in the **Details** panel. Now rename the second variable to `Damage`, set its type to **Float**, and ensure that it is set to be editable. Finally, set the **Damage** variable's default value to `0.3`.

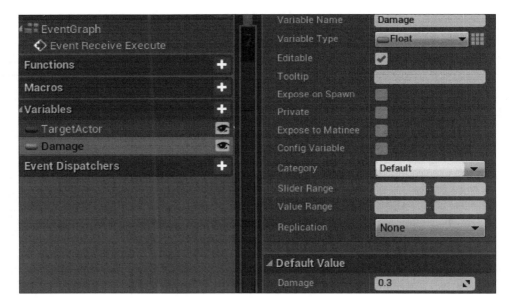

With the variables created, look at the event graph of the task. We first want to grab the target actor variable, where we will later store a reference to the player. To begin, place an **Event Receive Execute** node. Now drag a wire from the output execution pin of the event node to the graph, and search for `IsValid` in the search box. Attach the **IsValid** node under the **Utilities** category to the event node.

Add a **Get Blackboard Value as Actor** node to the graph. Drag the **Target Actor** variable onto the **Key** input pin of **Get Blackboard Value as Actor**. Then, connect the **Return Value** output pin to the **Input Object** input pin of the **IsValid** node. Attach an **Apply Damage** node to the **Is Valid** output execution pin of the **IsValid** node. Next, establish how much damage is done on each attack by dragging the **Damage** variable onto the **Base Damage** input pin of the **Apply Damage** node. Connect the **Return Value** output pin to the **Damaged Actor** input pin of **Apply Damage** to establish the target of the damage. Finally, conclude the task by attaching a **Finish Execute** node to the **Apply Damage** node, and checking the box next to the **Success** input. After applying a descriptive comment around this group of nodes, your final result should look like the following screenshot:

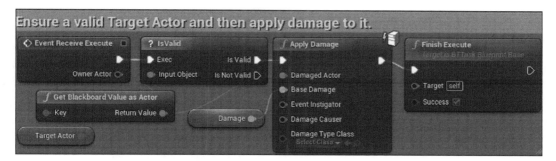

With the custom attack task created, return to the Behavior Tree. Because we are creating this attack as a melee attack, we want the enemy to perform the attack only after reaching the player. Find the **Attack Player** sequence node in **Behavior Tree**, drag a wire down from the bottom of the node, and add a new **DoAttackTask** task node between the **Move To** and **Wait** task nodes, which already exist, as shown here:

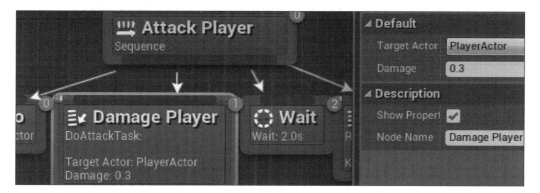

Click on the **DoAttackTask** node, and change the **Target Actor** selection in the **Details** panel to PlayerActor. You can also change **Node Name** to Damage Player to add some descriptive details to your use of the task. With our Behavior Tree set up to use our custom task that applies damage, we should be in a good position to test our work. However, if you compile, save, and test, you will find that the health meter does not appear to be affected when the enemy closes in on you, despite the damage being applied. To fix this, we must add an event to change the health meter when damage is dealt. Go to **Content Browser**, navigate to the **Blueprints** folder, and open **FirstPersonCharacter**.

Updating the health meter

Recall that in previous chapters, we linked the meters that are displayed on our HUD to variables contained within **FirstPersonCharacter**. In order to show the health meter decreasing in response to taking damage, we must decrease the player health variable each time damage is received. We will also want to ensure that the player health can never go below 0 to avoid potential bugs that an unexpected negative health value might cause. The end result will look like the following screenshot:

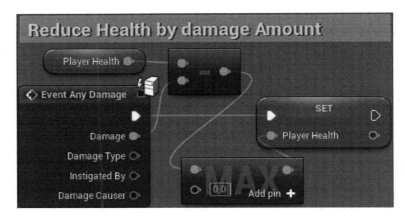

Begin by adding the **Event Any Damage** event node to empty graph space. Drag the **Player Health** variable onto the graph and use it to create a **Get Player Health** node. Attach this variable node to a **Float - Float** node. Now drag a wire from the **Damage** output pin of the event node, and attach it to the bottom input pin of the **Float - Float** node.

To ensure that the health value never goes below 0, drag a wire from the output pin of the **Float - Float** node and attach it to a **Max (Float)** node. Leave the bottom input field at its default value of 0.0. This node will return the higher of the two values given as inputs, such that if the calculated health ever goes below the lowermost value of 0.0, it will return 0.0 rather than the player health calculated after damage is subtracted. Finally, connect the output pin of the **Max (Float)** node to a **Set Player Health** node to adjust the variable value, and thus the health meter display.

Select all of these nodes and create a comment that describes the functionality. Then compile, save, and press **Play** to test. You should now notice the player health meter depleting when an enemy gets within range of the player and stops to attack.

Making enemies hear and investigate sounds

Now that our enemy is attacking the player, we want to give some additional attention to the means by which the enemy can detect the player. Enemies that can only pursue players who walk directly in front of them can easily be avoided. To address this, we will take advantage of our **PawnSensing** component to have the enemy detect nearby sounds that the player makes. If the player makes a sound within the detection range of an enemy, the enemy will walk to the location of that sound to investigate. If they catch the player in their sight, they will make an attempt to attack. Otherwise, they will wait at the location of the sound for a moment before returning to their patrol.

Adding hearing to the Behavior Tree

The first step to introducing any additional functionality to the AI is figuring out where that logic will fit within the Behavior Tree. Go to \ **Content Browser**, open the **Enemy** folder, and open **EnemyBehavior**. We are contemplating adding a sequence of events that occur when the enemy hears a sound. We want the enemy to continue attacking the player once they see them, so investigating a sound should be of a lower priority on the Behavior Tree. Move the **Attack Player** sequence and all of its task nodes further to the left in the Behavior Tree, leaving room between **Attack Player** and **Move to Patrol**. This is where we will add our hearing sequence. Drag a wire down from the **Selector** node, and attach it to a new **Sequence** node. Rename this node to Investigate Sound.

To have an enemy investigate the point where it heard a sound, we will need to keep track of two bits of information. The first is whether or not a sound has been heard. The second is the location that the sound came from, and thus the location that the enemy AI should investigate. We will create two keys within the Blackboard to store this information. Click on the **Blackboard** tab of **EnemyBehavior**.

Next, click on the **New Key** button, and choose to make a key of the **Vector** type. Call this key LocationOfSound. Click on **New Key** a second time, this time making it a **Bool** type, and call it HasHeardSound. With the keys created, click on the **Behavior Tree** tab to return to the Behavior Tree view.

Before we begin creating tasks, we can set up the condition that will determine when the investigation of a sound should take place. To do this, right-click on the **Investigate Sound** sequence node, hover over **Add Decorator**, and click on the **Blackboard** option. Now click on the blue decorator, and look at the **Details** panel. Under **Flow Control**, change the **Observer aborts** value to **Lower Priority**. This will ensure that the investigation can begin as soon as a sound is heard, even if the enemy is midway through a patrol task, by aborting the lower priority tasks. Now look at the **Blackboard** category and change **Blackboard Key** to **HasHeardSound**. Combined with **Key Query** being **Is Set**, this will allow the **Investigate Sound** sequence tasks to fire only when a sound has actually been heard. Finally, name the node something representative. I suggest Heard Sound?.

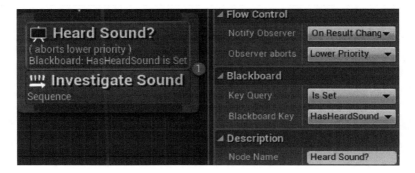

Setting up the investigating tasks

With the decorator set, we can move on to creating some of the tasks we will use to cause the enemy to investigate the location of the sound. The first action of our investigation sequence will be to move the enemy to the location of the sound. We have already done something very similar in the attack sequence. Drag a wire down from the **Investigate Sound** sequence, and attach it to a **Move To** task node.

In the **Details** panel of the **Move To** node, change **Blackboard Key** to **LocationOfSound**. Now drag a second wire down and attach it to a **Wait** node. Change **Wait Time** to 4 seconds and **Random Deviation** to 1 second. This will cause the enemy to move to the location of the sound that it heard, and wait at that location for 3 to 5 seconds, looking for the player.

Once the enemy is finished waiting at the investigation location, we want to reset the **Boolean** key that contains the information that a sound was heard. We do this so that when a new sound is heard, the key can be set to true one more time, causing another investigation to occur. We have already created a custom task called **ResetValueTask**. We need another task that does a similar job, but is capable of resetting a Boolean value.

Click on the **New Task** button at the top of the Behavior Tree, and select the **BTTask_BlueprintBase** option from the drop-down menu that appears. Return to **Content Browser** and find the new task object called **BTTask_BlueprintBase_New** in the **Enemy** folder. Rename this object to `ResetBoolTask`. Double-click on **ResetBoolTask** to return to the task's tab. We will be assembling sets of Blueprint logic to handle cases where we need to reset the variable telling the AI that a sound was heard. The Blueprint nodes that we will construct can be seen in the following screenshot:

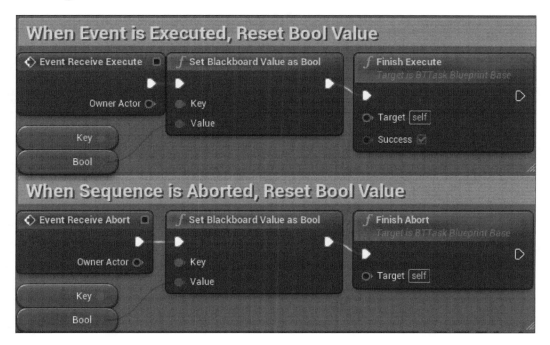

Look at the **My Blueprint** panel and add two variables. Call the first variable `Key` and change its type to **BlackboardKeySelector**. Rename the second variable to `Bool` and change its type to **Boolean**. Finally, ensure that both of these variables have the **Editable** box checked.

Now let's add the behavior for the task. Add an **Event Receive Execute** trigger node to the event graph. Drag a wire out from the execution pin and attach a **Set Blackboard Value as Bool** node. Next, drag the **Key** variable onto the **Key** input pin. Then, drag the Bool variable onto the **Value** input pin. Finally, drag a wire from the output execution pin of the **Set Blackboard Value as Bool** node, and attach it to a **Finish Execute** node. Check the box next to the **Success** input of this node.

In addition to handling the execution event, we will also have to address what happens when the hearing sequence in the Behavior Tree is aborted by the higher priority execution of the attack sequence. Even if the hearing sequence is aborted while in progress, we still need to ensure that the **HasHeardSound** variable is reset.

Add an **Event Receive Abort** trigger node to the graph, and attach it to another **Set Blackboard Value as Bool** node. As before, drag the **Key** variable onto the **Key** input pin and the **Bool** variable to the **Value** input pin. Finally, drag a wire from the output execution pin of the **Set Blackboard Value as Bool** node, and attach it to a **Finish Abort** node. Save the task and return to **EnemyBehavior**.

Drag a wire down and place a **ResetBoolTask** task node to the right of the **Wait** node. Change the **Key** selection to **HasHeardSound** inside the **Details** panel of **ResetBoolTask**. You should also change **Node Name** to `Reset Player Heard` in order to be more specific about its functionality. The final sequence of tasks should look like this screenshot:

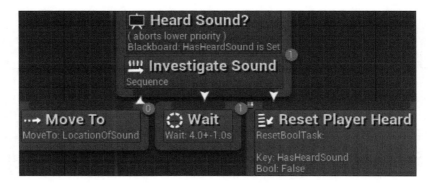

Interpreting and storing the noise event data

The **PawnSensing** component we added to **EnemyController** gives us the foundation to build both visual and auditory sensing in our enemy AI. Thus, we want to return to **EnemyController** and add some Blueprints that will instruct our AI how to react to the sounds in the world around them. Go to **Content Browser**, open the **Enemy** folder, and then open **EnemyController**.

In the **Components** panel, click on the **PawnSensing** object, and then use either the search function or the **Events** section of the **Details** panel to add an **OnHearNoise (PawnSensing)** node. This node will activate any time the **PawnSensing** component attached to **EnemyController** detects a special kind of sound broadcast by a pawn noise emitter. We will have to set up the Blueprint such that the enemies only detect noises that are made a short distance away. Otherwise, it would feel unfair for the player to shoot their gun from the opposite corner of the map and let every enemy instantly know their location.

Attach a **Branch** node to the **OnHearNoise (PawnSensing)** node. Before continuing with the nodes that will store the data about the noise event, we will first check whether the noise has occurred close enough to the enemy to trigger our investigate action. To evaluate this, we have to compare the location of the noise event detected and the location of the enemy. We will accomplish this by setting up the vector comparison shown in the following screenshot:

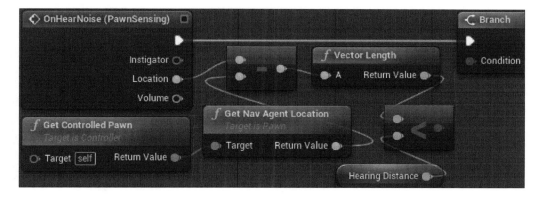

To figure out the location of the enemy doing the listening, create a **Get Controlled Pawn** node. Then drag a wire out from the **Return Value** output pin and attach it to a **Get Nav Agent Location** node. These two nodes will output the location of the pawn object controlled by the AI controller we are currently editing.

We want to subtract the vector location of the enemy from the vector location of the noise to get our distance, so drag a wire from the **Location** output pin of **OnHearNoise (PawnSensing)**, and attach it to a **Vector - Vector** node. Next, connect the bottom input pin of the **Vector - Vector** node to the **Return Value** output pin of **Get Nav Agent Location**. Drag a wire from the output pin of the **Vector - Vector** node, and attach it to a **Vector Length** node. This will translate the vector length to a float number.

We can now evaluate whether the float number calculated is less than the threshold distance we want to define for the enemy's hearing range. Drag a wire from the **Return Value of the Vector Length** node, and attach it to a **Float < Float** node. Remember that, as with any arbitrary value that defines a property, you can create a variable here to replace the number field and make it easier to adjust your threshold at a later time. To do so, create a new variable of the float type, and give it a default value that matches the number you want. I called this variable `HearingDistance` and gave it a value of `1600`, which worked well for the layout of my level. You may need to adjust this value to be appropriate for your map and intended gameplay. Attach your variable to the bottom input pin of the **Float < Float** node, or just type in the value.

To complete the condition, attach the output pin of **Float < Float** to the **Condition** input pin of the **Branch** node. This completes the steps we need to ensure that the sound being heard is within the range to act upon. Now we need to store the data about that sound in our Blackboard so that the Behavior Tree can access it. The Blueprint nodes needed to accomplish this can be seen in the following screenshot:

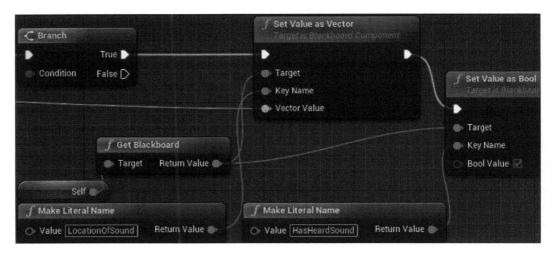

Start by dragging a wire from the **True** output execution pin of the **Branch** node, and attach it to a **Set Value as Vector** node. We need to fill in the three inputs for this node to store data about our sound location. First, drag a wire from the **Target** input pin, and attach it to a **Get Blackboard** node. Then drag a wire from the **Target** input of **Get Blackboard**, and attach it to a **Self** node. Next, drag a wire from the **Key Name** input of **Set Value as Vector**, and attach it to a **Make Literal Name** node. Type LocationOfSound in the **Value** input, as we want to store the vector location in the corresponding key in the Blackboard. Finally, drag a wire all the way from the **Location** output pin of the **OnHearNoise (Pawn Sensing)** event node to the **Vector Value** input pin of the **Set Value as Vector** node.

The last thing we need to do is store the information that a sound has been heard in the Blackboard. Drag the output execution pin of **Set Value as Vector** out and attach it to a **Set Value as Bool** node. Drag a second wire from the **Return Value** output pin of the **Get Blackboard** node you used earlier to the **Target** input pin of **Set Value as Bool**. Now drag a wire from the **Key Name** input pin out, and attach it to a new **Make Literal Name** node. Inside this **Value** input, type HasHeardSound. Finally, ensure that the **Bool Value** checkbox input of **Set Value as Bool** is checked in order to designate that a sound has been heard. Wrap this entire series of nodes in a useful comment container, compile, and save your work.

Adding noise to the player's actions

Now that we have modified our enemy AI to be able to detect sounds that are broadcast to the listener, we need to create the Blueprint nodes that will trigger the hearing response and attach them to player actions. This will give us the opportunity to introduce additional risk-versus-reward choices. If firing the gun to take out an enemy has the potential of alerting all nearby enemies of the player's presence and location, then the player might think twice about choosing to open fire on the enemy until they are sure that they have the advantage.

The **PawnSensing** component of **EnemyController** is able to detect noise only if it is created from **PawnNoiseEmitter**. The existing sound effect that we play when the player fires their gun will not trigger the enemy **PawnSensing** component. It is important to know that the nodes that produce noise for pawn sensing have no direct relationship with the sound a player hears. The noise exists only in terms of producing an event that the AI can hear and respond to.

Open **FirstPersonCharacter** from the **Blueprints** folder under **Content Browser**. Click on the **Add Component** button and add **PawnNoiseEmitter**. This component must be added to an actor in order for noises it broadcasts to be detected by a pawn sensor. We will now change two player abilities to produce detectable noise utilizing this component, namely sprinting and shooting.

We will begin by adding noise to sprinting. We could have attached our noise-producing node at the end of the block of nodes that triggers a sprint. However, that would produce noise only one time per button push. Sprinting should logically produce noise upon every footfall, as a repeated event, for as long as the player is actively sprinting. Since we are actively draining the stamina of the player while they are holding down the sprint button, we also have the opportunity to repurpose this drain function to also repeatedly produce noise.

Start by finding the block of nodes that begins with the **Sprint Drain** custom event. Drag a wire from the execution output pin of the **Set Player Stamina** node, and attach it to a **Make Noise (PawnNoiseEmitter)** node. It is important that you choose the version of **Make Noise** that is produced from the **PawnNoiseEmitter** component, indicated by PawnNoiseEmitter showing in parentheses next to the node name in the **Executable actions** search window. Only this version of the node will produce noise that is detectable by the **PawnSensing** component of **Enemy Controller**.

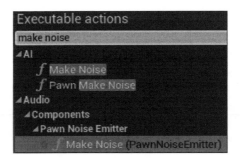

With **Make Noise (PawnNoiseEmitter)** connected, drag a wire out from the **Noise Location** input pin and attach it to a **Get Actor Location** node. Then drag a wire from the **Noise Maker** input pin of **Make Noise (PawnNoiseEmitter)**, and attach it to a **Self** node. Finally, change the **Loudness** input field to 1. After editing the comment around these nodes to reflect the new functionality, the final result should look like this screenshot:

Next, we want to find the block of nodes that handles spawning of the projectile when the player fires the gun. In *Chapter 3, Creating Screen UI Elements*, we added a few nodes to the end of this sequence. They reduced the ammo count every time a shot was fired. Find the **Set Player Current Ammo** node, and drag a wire from its output execution pin to a **Make Noise (PawnNoiseEmitter)** node. Mimicking the steps followed for the sprint noise, attach a **Self** node to the **Noise Maker** input pin, attach a **Get Actor Location** node to the **Noise Location** input pin, and set the **Loudness** input to 1. You have the option to use a second wire from the **Return Value** output pin of the existing **Get Actor Location** node attached to **Play Sound at Location**, rather than create a redundant node. This is shown in the next screenshot:

Compile, save, and click on **Play** to test your work. While behind an enemy or otherwise outside their line of sight, sprinting or firing your gun should result in the enemy approaching the position you were in when you made the noise. If they establish line of sight with you during their investigation, they will begin heading directly toward you.

Making the enemies destructible

With detection possible with both sight and sound, you might now find it difficult to avoid being spotted by enemies. We will now turn our attention to the other side of gameplay balancing, and equip the player with the means of combating the enemies.

Saving time by reusing existing Blueprint content

Recall that in earlier chapters, we created enemy targets that the player could destroy after a couple of hits with a projectile. We want to give the player a similar ability to mitigate the threat provided by our new enemies. To do so, we can repurpose the Blueprint nodes we already created to handle damage taking and destruction.

Navigate to **Content Browser**, go inside the **Blueprints** folder, and open **CylinderTarget_Blueprint**. In the **Event Graph**, find the sequence of nodes that are triggered by the **Event Hit** node. Click and drag a selection box around every node in this sequence, ensuring that you don't miss any connected nodes. With all the nodes in this sequence selected, right-click on any one of the nodes and select the **Copy** option, as shown here:

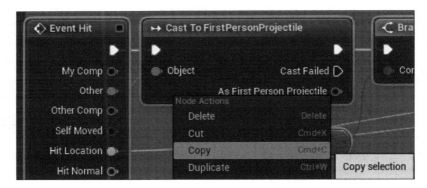

With the nodes copied, return to the **Content Browser** and open **EnemyCharacter** inside the **Enemy** folder. Navigate sufficiently far away from other nodes to give yourself plenty of room, and then click on the *Ctrl* (PC) or *command* (Mac) plus *V* keys to paste the previously copied Blueprint nodes in this event graph. If you try compiling now, you will see a few errors and warnings appear on some of the nodes, as seen in the following screenshot:

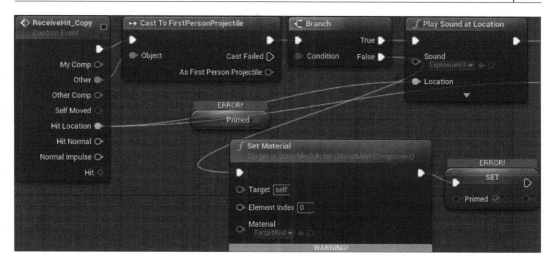

The errors you see are present on nodes that relied on components and properties of the target cylinder Blueprint but to which we no longer have access inside the **EnemyCharacter** Blueprint, most notably the **Primed** variable. The concept of priming an enemy before defeating them doesn't translate well in humanoid enemies anyway, so delete the **Get Primed** and **Set Primed** nodes, as well as the **Set Material** node attached to the False output execution pin of the **Branch** node. We will be replacing the primed concept with a more traditional health tracking system.

We will need a variable to track enemy health as damage is applied. From the **My Blueprint** panel, create a new variable called **EnemyHealth**. Change its type to **Integer**, and check the **Editable** box. Finally, change its default value to the number of hits you would like each enemy to take before being killed. In my example, I chose to set this value to 3. Next, we will use this variable to check whether a hit should destroy the enemy or simply reduce its health by one. The nodes used to handle this branch logic are shown in this screenshot:

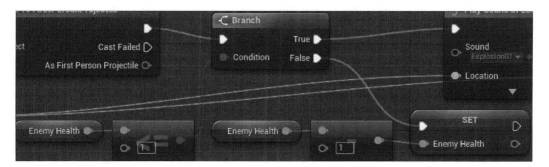

First, we need to determine the conditional node that will branch whether or not an enemy is destroyed by a hit. Because we will want the enemy to be destroyed when they reach zero health, we can make a comparison between the existing enemy health, and the integer 1. Moreover, because this evaluation happens before health is reduced, and each hit is going to reduce health by one, we know that receiving a hit with 1 health or less remaining will result in the enemy health being 0.

Put this reasoning into practice by finding the **Branch** node that is led to by the **Cast to FirstPersonProjectile** node. Drag a wire from the **Condition** input of this node, and attach it to an **Int <= Int** node. Drag the **EnemyHealth** variable onto the top input pin of this node, and type 1 in the bottom input field.

Next, we need to decrease **EnemyHealth** by 1 each time the enemy is hit with a shot but is not destroyed. Drag a wire from the **False** output execution pin of the **Branch** node, and attach it to a **Set Enemy Health** node. Now connect the **Enemy Health** input pin to an **Int - Int** node. Finally, drag the **EnemyHealth** variable onto the top input pin of **Int - Int**, and type 1 in the bottom input field.

From now on, when the player shoots an enemy a number of times equal to the value given to **EnemyHealth**, they will explode and be destroyed similarly to how the cylinder targets behaved in earlier chapters. Compile, save, and press **Play** to see this in action.

Spawning more enemies during gameplay

Now that we are able to destroy enemies, we need to again ramp up the difficulty for the player. To do so, we are going to spawn new enemies in the level as the player is playing the game. In this way, the game can continue if the player destroys the first few enemies, and if they are too slow to defeat enemies, the difficulty will gradually increase.

Choosing a spawn point where enemies will appear

First, we must decide where our enemies will be spawning in the level. We will be spawning enemies in random spots within a circular distance from an object placed in the level. Return to the level editor by clicking on the **FirstPersonExampleMap** tab. Find the **PatrolPoint1** object in the **World Outliner** panel. Duplicate the object by right-clicking on it, selecting **Edit**, and then selecting **Duplicate**. Rename the new object to SpawnPoint. Move the **SpawnPoint** object close to the center of your level, ensuring that it is located a bit off the ground in a player- and enemy-accessible area.

We will be placing the Blueprint nodes that will create new enemies inside the **Level Blueprint**. A Level Blueprint is a special Blueprint that is tied to the entire level, serving as a global event graph. They are especially well suited for setting up level-specific items, such as enemy placements and door behavior. To edit the Level Blueprint, click on the **Blueprints** button in the level editor toolbar and select the **Open Level Blueprint** option.

Managing spawn rates and limits with variables

Rather than relying on the placement of enemies in a level on a set patrol, we are going to be gradually spawning those enemies in the level to present a more aggressive threat to the player. As a consequence, we will want to set up our spawning logic to trigger repeatedly in a loop, with the time between spawns determined by a variable. In the **My Blueprint** panel, add a new variable called SpawnTime. Set its type to **Float**, make it editable, and set the default value to 10.0 for a 10-second spawn rate.

In addition to setting the spawn rate, we will also want some form of limiter on the spawning of enemies. Without this, an enemy would spawn every 10 seconds until the game ends, potentially filling the map with dozens of enemies. To prevent this, we will create an additional variable to set a cap on the number of enemies. Create another variable and call it MaxEnemies. Set the variable type to **Integer** and make it editable. I set the default value of **MaxEnemies** to 5, but you can set the number as high or as low as you think is the appropriate maximum number of enemies that your level can support.

In order for **MaxEnemies** to function as a cap on the number of enemies present in the level, we need a way of keeping track of the current number of enemies. To do this, we will temporarily leave the Level Blueprint, and instead open the **FirstPersonCharacter** Blueprint, found in the **Blueprints** folder of **Content Browser**. Inside **FirstPersonCharacter**, create a new variable called CurrentEnemyCount. Set its type to **Integer** and ensure that **Editable** is checked.

> Level Blueprints can receive information from other Blueprints through casting, but there is no easy way to get information stored in a Level Blueprint and use it in other Blueprints. As a consequence, any variable you make that is likely to be affected by actions in other Blueprints, such as the **CurrentEnemyCount** variable, is better placed outside of the Level Blueprint. In this case, we are storing it with the rest of our game data information on the player object.

Now that we have a variable to track the current enemy count, we need to decrease this value whenever an enemy is destroyed. Recall that the Blueprint nodes managing enemy destruction are located in the **EnemyCharacter** Blueprint. Open the **Enemy** folder in **Content Browser**, and then open the **EnemyCharacter** Blueprint.

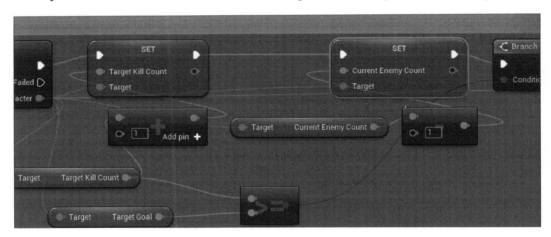

In the **EnemyCharacter** Blueprint, locate the series of nodes that are triggered by the **the Event Hit** node. Near the end of this node sequence, find the **Cast to FirstPersonCharacter** node. Create some additional space between the **Set Target Kill Count** node and the **Branch** node, and break the connection between their input and output execution nodes. Drag a wire out from the **As First Person Character** output pin of **Cast to FirstPersonCharacter**, and attach it to a **Set Current Enemy Count** node. Drag a wire from this node's **Current Enemy Count** input pin to an **Int - Int** node.

Now drag another wire from the **As First Person Character** output pin of **Cast to FirstPersonCharacter,** and attach it to a **Get Current Enemy Count** node. Attach this node to the top input pin of the **Int - Int** node, and fill in the bottom input field with 1. Next, connect the **Set Target Kill Count** node to the input execution pin of **Set Current Enemy Count.** Finally, connect the output execution pin of this node to the **Branch** node.

Now that we have established variables to determine the spawn rate and cap the number of enemies in a level, we should return to the Level Blueprint. Click on the tab with a Blueprint icon that is labeled **FirstPersonExampleMap.**

Spawning new enemies in the Level Blueprint

Back in the Level Blueprint, turn your attention to the event graph. We will want to initiate the spawning logic as soon as the game is played and in a loop after every few seconds at a rate determined by the **SpawnTime** variable. Add an **Event Begin Play** node to the event graph, and attach it to a **Set Timer** node. Drag the **SpawnTime** variable onto the **Time** input pin, and check the box next to the **Looping** input pin. Finally, type Spawn inside the **Function Name** input field. We will be creating a custom **Spawn** function that will be called on each pass through this loop. Remember to create a comment around these nodes as a reminder to the function of this loop.

Now add a **Custom Event** node to empty grid space by searching for and selecting **Add Custom Event...,** and rename the node to Spawn. Drag a wire from the **Spawn** node and attach it to a **Cast to FirstPersonCharacter** node. Now attach the output execution pin of this node to a **Branch** node.

Drag a wire out from the **Object** input node of **Cast to FirstPersonCharacter**, and attach it to a **Get Player Character** node. Then, drag a wire from the **As First Person Character** output pin, and attach it to a **Get Current Enemy Count** node. Drag out the **Current Enemy Count** output pin of this node and attach it to an **Int < Int** node. Next, drag the **MaxEnemies** variable onto the bottom input pin of this node. Finally, drag a wire out from the **Condition** input pin of the **Branch** node, and attach it to the **Int < Int** node's output pin. Your nodes should now match the following screenshot:

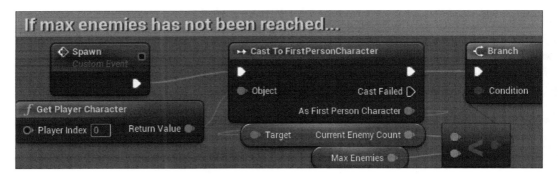

The next step is to actually spawn an enemy. To do this, drag a wire out from the **True** output execution pin of the **Branch** node, and attach it to a **Spawn AIFrom Class** node. This node is custom built to spawn new AI objects, and requires you to designate a pawn and a Behavior Tree. Select **Enemy Character** from the drop-down menu on the **Pawn Class** input pin, and select **EnemyBehavior** for the **Behavior Tree** input. Now we need to get random locations and rotations for the remaining inputs of this node. The Blueprint nodes used to accomplish this can be seen in this screenshot:

Start by switching tabs back to the level editor. Inside the **World Outliner** panel of **FirstPersonExampleMap**, click on the **SpawnPoint** object so that it is highlighted. With **SpawnPoint** selected, return to the **Level Blueprint** tab. Far to the left of the other nodes, right-click in empty grid space, ensure that **Context Sensitive** is checked, and select the **Create a Reference to SpawnPoint** option. Attach the node that appears to a **Get Actor Location** node. Then, attach the **Return Value** output pin of this node to a **Get Random Point in Radius** node.

Get Random Point in Radius takes a location as an input and returns a random location within a designated distance away as an output. Set the **Radius** input of this node to a high number. I found 1000.0 to be an appropriate number to make the most of my level available for spawning. Attach the **Return Value** output pin to the **Location** input of the **Spawn AIFrom Class** node.

Next, drag a wire from the **Rotation** input pin of **Spawn AIFrom Class**, and attach it to a **Make Rot** node. This node converts three **Float** inputs into a rotation value. We only want to choose a random rotation for our spawned enemies in the **Yaw** axis, so drag a wire from the **Yaw** input pin and attach it to a **Random Float** node. The final input for the **Spawn AIFrom Class** node, **No Collision Fail**, enables or disables a built-in check to see whether or not the intended spawn location of the actor is blocked by the collision of another object. If the check fails, which means that the actor would be spawned partially inside another object, the actor will fail to spawn. Since we want to ensure that our enemies are not spawning inside other objects, we will leave this input unchecked, ensuring that this test happens. Create a comment container around this series of nodes, describing its utility for finding random rotation and locations near the spawnpoint object.

The final step is to increase the enemy count each time an enemy is spawned. Drag a second wire out from the **Cast to FirstPersonController** node, and attach it to a **Set Current Enemy Count** node. Move this node to the right of the **Spawn AIFrom Class** node, and connect the two execution pins. Now drag a second wire out from the **Get Current Enemy Count** node near the casting node, and attach it to an **Int + Int** node. Change the bottom input field to 1, and move the node to the right of **Spawn AIFrom Class**. Attach the output pin of the **Int + Int** node to the **Current Enemy Count** pin of the **Set Current Enemy Count** node.

After adding a descriptive comment to these nodes, the result should look like this:

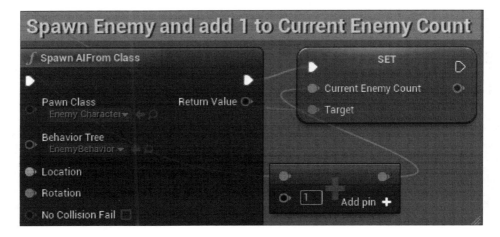

Compile, save, and click on **Play** to test your enemy spawning. Based on what you have set your spawn rate to and where you have placed your spawn point, you should regularly see new enemies appear as you run the game. You will notice, however, that the enemies are not moving once spawned unless they hear or see the player. This is because they are not being created with an established patrol point to pursue. Rather than adding patrol points to our spawned enemies, we will be taking our new appreciation of randomness and adding it to our enemy navigation behavior.

Creating enemy wandering behavior

Previously, we set the default behavior for enemies as a patrolling movement between two points. While this worked well as a test bed for our hearing and seeing components, and would be appropriate for a stealth-oriented game, we are going to ramp up the challenge and action of this game's experience by replacing this behavior with random wandering. This will make avoiding enemies significantly harder, encouraging more direct confrontations. To do this, we are going to return to the **EnemyBehavior** Behavior Tree. Open **EnemyBehavior** from the **Enemy** folder in the **Content Browser**.

Identifying a wander point with a custom task

Once you've opened **EnemyBehavior**, click on the **Blackboard** tab. We need to create a key that will store the location of the next destination that the enemy should wander to. Unlike the **PatrolPoint** key, our destination won't be represented by an in-game actor, but rather by vector coordinates. Create a new key in the **Blackboard** panel now, and call this key **WanderPoint**. Change **Key Type** to **Vector**. Now click on the **Behavior Tree** tab to return to the Behavior Tree.

In the Behavior Tree, we can remove two of the sequences we have already established to handle moving between patrol points and idling. Select the **Patrol** and **Idle** sequence nodes, along with their attached task nodes, and delete them. Now drag a wire out from the **Selector** node and attach it to a new **Sequence** node. Rename this node to wander, and move this node to the right of both the **Attack Player** and **Investigate Sound** sequences.

The first task of our wander sequence will be to determine where in the level the enemy should be wandering. For this, we will need to create another custom task. Click on the **New Task** button and select the **BTTask_BlueprintBase** option from the drop-down menu. Return to **Content Browser** and find the new task object called **BTTask_BlueprintBase_New** in the **Enemy** folder. Rename this task object to FindWanderPointTask. Double-click on **FindWanderPointTask** to open the **Event Graph** editor for the new task.

We will be setting up nodes that will grab the location of the enemy actor and generate a random point within a radius around that location. This point will then be stored as our wander point. The nodes used to accomplish this can be seen in the following screenshot:

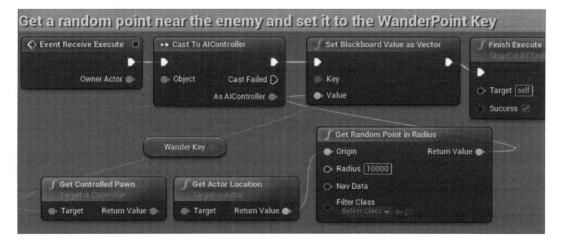

First, we need to create a variable within this task that will allow us to establish a reference to a **Blackboard Key**. Add a new variable and call it WanderKey. Set the type to **BlackboardKeySelector** and make sure that the **Editable** checkbox is selected.

Now add an **Event Receive Execute** node to the event graph. Drag a wire from the **Owner Actor** output pin and attach it to a **Cast to AIController** node. Then attach the two nodes' execution pins. Now that we have access to the AI Controller, we can access its controlled actor's location. Drag a wire out from the **As AIController** output pin of the casting node, and attach it to a **Get Controlled Pawn** node. Next, drag a wire out from the **Return Value** output pin of this node, and attach it to a **Get Actor Location** node.

With the enemy actor location in hand, we can now generate the random location that will serve as our wander point. Drag a wire out from the **Return Value** output pin of **Get Actor Location**, and attach it to a **Get Random Point in Radius** node. Set the **Radius** value of this node to a large number that should cover most or all of your level. I set mine to 10000.

Next, we need to store this vector in the Blackboard. Drag a wire out from the **Return Value** output of **Get Random Point in Radius**, and attach it to a **Set Blackboard Value as Vector** node. Drag the **WanderKey** variable onto the **Key** input of this node, and then attach the input execution pin to the output execution pin of the **Cast To AIController** node. Finally, drag a wire out from the output execution pin of **Set Blackboard Value as Vector**, attach it to a **Finish Execute Node**, and check the **Success** input box.

Add a descriptive comment around these nodes. Then compile and save this Blueprint. Click on the **EnemyBehavior** tab to return to the Behavior Tree.

Adding wandering to the Behavior Tree

Now that we have our custom task, we can make the task sequence that will cause the enemy to find a wander point, move to it, and wait there for a brief period of time.

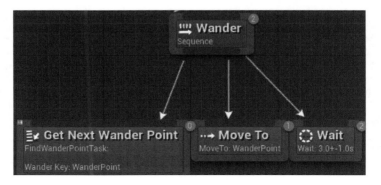

Start by dragging a wire out from the **Wander** sequence node, and attach it to your new **FindWanderPointTask** task node. Click on the new node and change **Wander Key** in the **Details** panel to **WanderPoint**. Also change **Node Name** to Get Next Wander Point to be more explicit about its purpose. Then compile the Blueprint to see the change in the node.

Drag another wire down from the **Wander** sequence node, and attach it to a **MoveTo** task node. Click on this node and change **Blackboard Key** to WanderPoint. Move this node to the right of the **Get Next Wander Point** node. Drag a third wire down and attach it to a **Wait** task node, placing the node to the right of those other two task nodes. In the **Details** panel, change **Wait Time** to 3.0 and **Random Deviation** to 1.0 to give the wait time a bit of variance. Now compile and save the Behavior Tree.

A few final modifications should be made before we test our work. Return to the level editor by clicking on **FirstPersonExampeMap**. Any enemies you have manually placed in the world can now be removed, as we now have an enemy spawner to serve the function of creating our enemies. Find the enemy actors in **World Outliner** and delete them by right-clicking on the object, selecting **Edit**, and then selecting **Delete**. Now find the **FirstPersonCharacter** object and select it. In the **Details** panel, scroll down until you see a list of the variables we attached to the character Blueprint. Unless you created a custom category for these variables, they will be listed under the **Default** category. From here, we can easily modify the game values that determine player behavior and our win conditions. In this case, we want to modify the **Target Goal** value to be higher so that the game can continue for a longer period of time. I set this value to 20 so that the player must eliminate 20 enemies before winning the game:

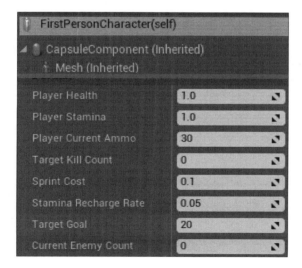

Now click on **Play** to run the game. You should see the spawned enemies choosing paths in random directions and moving toward them. When an enemy reaches their wander point, they will pause there briefly, before choosing another random point and walking there. You will also notice that the enemies choose wander points independent of one another. This is because each enemy has their own instance of the Behavior Tree. Thus, every Behavior Tree task, such as the one we just created to find a wander point, is running independently for each enemy. You will also notice that because we chose to have higher-priority sequences abort lower-priority sequences, anytime an enemy hears or sees the player, they will end their wander movement and begin approaching the player or the location of the sound.

Summary

In this chapter, we started off on the path of creating a challenging but balanced game experience by enhancing the capabilities of our AI-driven enemies. We gave our enemies zombie-like behavior by allowing them to wander aimlessly around the level until noticing the player by sight or sound. We also gave them the ability to charge forward when they notice the player and launch a melee attack, lowering the player's health. Then we gave the player the chance to fight back by attacking the enemy, eventually destroying them once the enemy's health is depleted. Finally, we gave new flexibility to our game by setting up a system to create new enemies as the game is being played.

At this point, the core content of our game is nearly complete. You should feel proud of the significant progress you have made! You can take some time to tweak the many variables you have created to customize the gameplay to your liking, or continue reading if you are ready to move on to the final systems. In the next chapter, we will be adding the last components necessary for a full game experience. We will end the game when the player runs out of health, create a round-based advancement system, and create a save system so that the player can return to a previously saved game state.

7
Tracking Game States and Applying Finishing Touches

In this chapter, we will be taking the final steps to evolve our game into a complete and fun experience that challenges the player. First, we will introduce player death, which is activated when the player's health is fully drained. Then, we will introduce a round system that will elevate the challenge for the player by requiring increasingly numerous enemies to be defeated as they progress through the rounds. Finally, we will introduce a *saving* and *loading* system so that the player can leave the game and later come back to the round they were last playing on. With these things accomplished, we will have an arcade-style first-person shooter that a player can continually return to for an increasingly difficult challenge. In the process, we will cover the following topics:

- Branching menus based on player conditions
- Creating scaling difficulty with gameplay modifiers
- Supporting the game state being saved and reloaded at a later time
- Branching level initialization based on the save data
- Creating transition screens that display gameplay data

Making danger real with player death

During the last chapter, we made significant progress towards a balanced game, in which enemies threaten the player but the player can use skill to overcome that challenge. One missing component glaringly remains. If the player runs out of health, they should not be able to continue progressing through the game. Instead, we will be taking our learning from the win screen we created, and applying it to a lose screen. This screen will enable the player to restart the level with full ammo and a freshly filled health bar, but will also negate any progress they had made toward reaching their target goal.

Setting up a lose screen

The lose screen will be presented when the player runs out of health. We will present them with options to restart the last round or quit the game. You may remember the win screen we created; we presented similar options there. Rather than remake the UI screen from scratch, we can save some time by using our WinMenu object as a template.

Go to the **Content Browser** and open the **UI** folder inside **FirstPersonBp**. Right-click on **WinMenu** and select the **Duplicate** option. Name this new Blueprint widget LoseMenu. Now open **LoseMenu** and select the text object showing **You Win**. Look at the **Details** panel, and change the **Text** field under **Content** to You Lose. Try Again?. Also change the **Color and Opacity** setting to a dark red color. Finally, you may wish to change the **Shadow Color** setting's alpha value from 0.0 to 1.0 to show shadows behind the text, as shown in this screenshot:

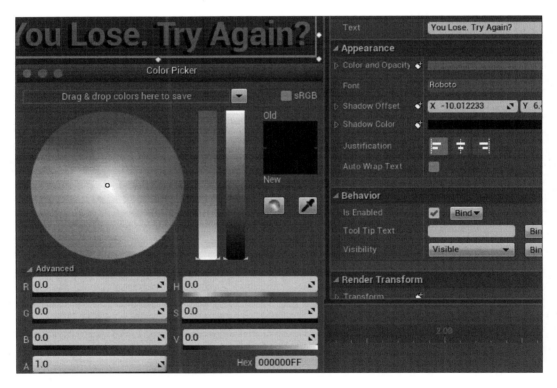

The two buttons can remain identical to their WinMenu counterparts in appearance and functionality for now. Compile and save this Blueprint, and then return to the **Content Browser**. Open **FirstPersonCharacter** inside the **Blueprints** folder.

To track whether or not the player has lost the game, we will need to create a new variable. From the **My Blueprint** panel, add a new variable called `LostGame`. In the **Details** panel, set **Variable Type** to **Boolean**. With the variable created, find the series of nodes we used to decrease the player's health, triggering off the **Event Any Damage** node.

We will need to extend the set player health operation with a branch comparison that will test whether the player's health is less than zero, and if so, set the `LostGame` variable to `false` and end the game. The nodes used to accomplish this are shown in the following screenshot:

Begin by giving yourself additional room to the right of the **Set Player Health** node. Drag a wire from the output execution pin of this node to a **Branch** node. Then connect the **Condition** input pin of the **Branch** node to a **Float >= Float** node. Leave the top input field of this new node as `0.0`, and connect the bottom input pin to the output pin of the **Set Player Health** node.

Now, drag a wire from the **True** output execution pin of the **Branch** node, and connect it to a **Set Lost Game** node. Check the **Lost Game** input pin box to set this Boolean to **True** when the player runs out of health. Then, connect the **Set Lost Game** node to an **End Game** node, which will call our previously created function to show the win menu. The next step will be to edit the **End Game** function so that it will show a lose menu if the function is called while the **LostGame** variable is set to **True**.

Find the block of nodes that triggers off the **End Game** event, where we call our **WinMenu** screen. After the nodes where we pause the game and enable the mouse arrow, we are going to create a branch node that will test the **LostGame** variable, as seen in the following screenshot:

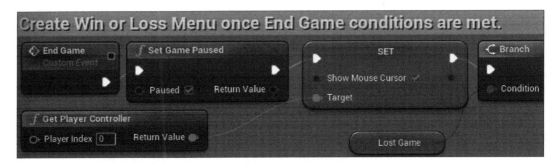

Start by breaking the connection between the **Set Show Mouse Cursor** and the **Create WinMenu_C Widget** nodes, and drag the widget and viewport nodes to the side for now. Then connect the **Set Show Mouse Cursor** node to a new **Branch** node. Next, drag the **LostGame** variable onto the **Condition** input pin of the **Branch** node. The next step will be to create and display **Lose Menu** when **LostGame** is **True** and **Win Menu** when it is **False**, as seen in this screenshot:

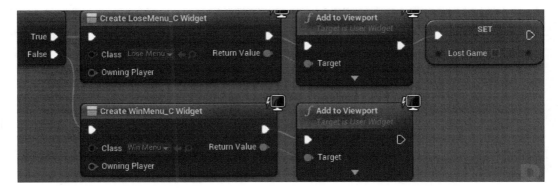

Drag a wire from the **True** output execution pin of the **Branch** node, and connect it to a new **Create Widget** node. Inside this node, select **Lose Menu** from the **Class** input drop-down menu. Then drag a wire from the **Return Value** output pin to an **Add to Viewport** node. Finish the **True** branch by attaching the viewport node to a **Set Lost Game** node, and ensure that the **Lost Game** input checkbox is left unchecked. This step is necessary to ensure that the game won't mistakenly think that the player has already lost if they restart or resume playing later. Finally, reconnect the create widget and viewport nodes you dragged aside earlier to the **False** output execution pin of the **Branch** node.

Compile, save, and click on **Play** to test your work. If you stand next to an enemy long enough for it to drain your health to zero, you should now see the lose menu we created.

Creating round-based scaling with saved games

We now have a game that supports a full play experience. The game can be won with the appropriate application of skill, but can also be lost by getting overwhelmed by the intelligent enemies we created. However, the gameplay experience is limited to the number of enemies we have set as our target goal. This results in the game feeling shallow. To address this, we can adopt techniques used by arcade games, which increase the difficulty of the game as the player progresses through a series of rounds. This is a way to add depth and fun to your game using the existing assets, without requiring the creation hours of custom content.

The rounds we create will serve as the score of the player. The higher the round they reach, the more the player is thought to have achieved. To ensure that the maximum round the player reaches is limited only by their skill, rather than the amount of time for which they play the game in a single setting, we will be implementing a *save system* so that the player can pick up from where they left off if they leave the game and come back to it later.

Storing game information using a SaveGame object

The first step we need to perform in order to create a save system is to create a new kind of Blueprint that will store the game data that we want to save. Go to the **Content Browser** and open the **Blueprints** folder. Click on the **Add New** button, select **Blueprints**, and then click on **Blueprint Class**. In the window that appears, search for and select **SaveGame** to create a new Blueprint of that class. Name this Blueprint SaveSystem, and double-click on it to open the Blueprint.

This Blueprint will contain our variable stored for the saved data:

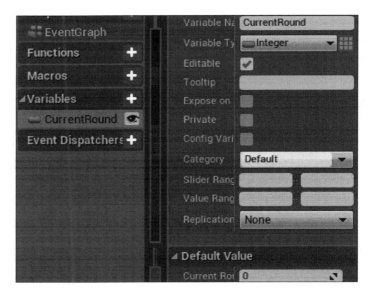

In our case, we are going to be implementing a series of increasingly difficult rounds, so we will want to track which round the player was on before they quit the game. We do not need to store any data on how many enemies the player has killed, because it would make more sense to the player for each game session to start at the beginning of a round. To track the current round, create a new variable called CurrentRound from the **My Blueprint** panel. Change **Variable Type** to **Integer**, mark the variable as **Editable**, and ensure that its default value is set to 0. That's all we need to do in SaveSystem. Compile and save the Blueprint now.

Storing and loading the saved data when starting the game

Now that we have a container for our saved data, we need to ensure that the data is stored somewhere on the player's machine, and that it is retrieved when the player returns to the game. We also want the saved data to be updated each time the level loads, because we will be increasing the current round number each time the player wins a round. Like the rest of our gameplay settings, we will be adding this process to the FirstPersonCharacter Blueprint. Go to the **Content Browser**, open the **Blueprints** folder, and open **FirstPersonCharacter** now.

In addition to the SaveSystem Blueprint, which will store information about what gameplay data to save, we are going to need a save game object that will actually contain the particular data for that user. To easily reference this save data, we will save it in a variable that we can reference throughout FirstPersonCharacter. From the **My Blueprint** panel, create a new variable called SaveGameInstance. In the **Details** panel, click on the **Variable Type** drop-down menu and search for Save System. Select the **Save System** option to allow this variable to contain an instance of the save system Blueprint that we just created, as shown in the following screenshot. This variable does not need to be editable, and you should leave the default value to **None**.

Now find the block of Blueprint nodes that draws the HUD on the screen when the gameplay begins, triggering off the **Event Begin Play** node. Similarly to what we did with the win menu sequence, break the connections between **Event Begin Play** and the **Create HUD_C** widget. Then drag the widget node and its connections to the side to make room for a significant number of new nodes. Back at the **Event Begin Play** node, drag a wire out from its output execution pin, and attach it to a **Does Save Game Exist** node.

When the game begins, we are going to use **Does Save Game Exist** to check for the existence of a "save game" file that features the save slot and user we specify in the node. We are going to be saving our data in a single save slot only, so each save operation will overwrite the previously saved data. Additionally, we will not be creating a user system for our game, so anyone playing the game on a particular machine will be assumed to be the only player. A Branch node will direct the game operations, depending on whether or not a saved game is found. If no saved game exists, a new save game object will be created. If one already exists, we will load the saved data from it.

The nodes used to accomplish this can be seen in this screenshot:

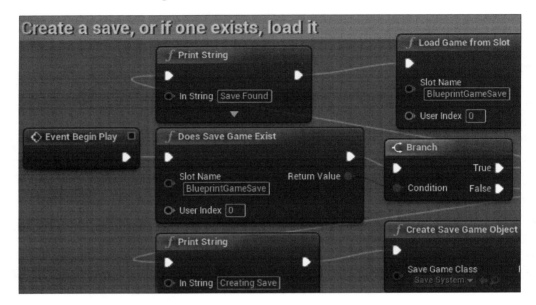

First, we must determine what our save game slot is going to be called. In the **Slot Name** input field of **Does Save Game Exist**, type `BlueprintGameSave`. Leave the **User Index** input at `0`. This combination asks the player whether there is a saved game by the first user in the user index, which will be our only user, and in the save slot called **BlueprintGameSave**, which will be our only save slot. Next, drag a wire from the **Return Value** output pin of **Does Save Game Exist**, and attach it to a **Branch** node.

 Whenever you are constructing a complex system, like our "save" structure, it is wise to use the **Print String** nodes, as shown in the previous screenshot, to evaluate during gameplay that your Blueprint logic is behaving the way you think it should. In the preceding case, we are finding out whether or not a saved game was found and printing the result.

From the **Branch** node, we will be creating a path to load content from a saved game, and another path to create a save game file. Drag a wire from the **True** output execution pin of the **Branch** node. If you wish to see a debug message printed on the screen when a saved game is supposed to be loaded, you can first route the **True** path of the **Branch** node through a **Print String** node, as seen in the preceding example. But this is not necessary to make the "save" system function. Whether or not you choose to use a **Print String** node, ensure that the **Branch** node is connected to a **Load Game from Slot** node, and enter **BlueprintGameSave** in the **Slot Name** input field.

Next, drag a wire from the **False** output execution pin of the **Branch** node. You again have the choice of attaching it to a **Print String** node to aid in debugging, or just attaching it directly to a **Create Save Game Object** node. Within this node, click on the **Save Game Class** input dropdown, and select **Save System** from the options presented.

Now we need to ensure that the save data, whether we just created it or are loading it from an existing file, is stored inside our SaveGameInstance variable. This can be accomplished through casting, as seen here:

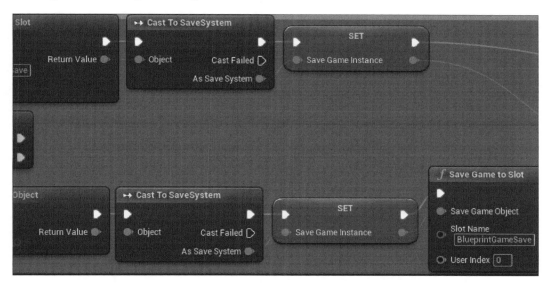

Start by dragging a wire from the **Return Value** output pin of the **Load Game from Slot** node, and attach it to a **Cast to SaveSystem** node. Also connect the execution pins of these two nodes. Then drag the **SaveGameInstance** variable onto the **As Save System** output pin of the casting node to both create and attach a **Set Save Game Instance** node.

Next, attach the same variable-data storing nodes in the branch where we are creating a new save game object. Drag a wire from the **Return Value** output pin of the **Create Save Game Object** node, and attach it to a new **Cast to SaveSystem** node. Connect the execution pins between these nodes, and then drag the **SaveGameInstance** variable onto the **As Save System** output pin of **Cast to SaveSystem**.

With our save game object created and stored in a variable, we need to save this data in a file that will be stored on the player's machine. Drag a wire from the output pin of the **Set Save Game Instance** node we just created, and drop it onto a **Save Game to Slot** node. Inside this node, enter `BlueprintGameSave` in the **Slot Name** input field. This will complete the steps necessary to create or load a save file when the game starts playing. Select all of these nodes and wrap them in a comment box to leave for yourself a note about their functionality.

Increasing the enemy target goal

Our next goal is to take advantage of the data we can store in the save file to change the gameplay for the player as they progress. We will do this by extracting the current round from the save file, and multiplying the number of enemies that need to be defeated to complete a round by a new multiplier variable we will create. This is shown in the following screenshot:

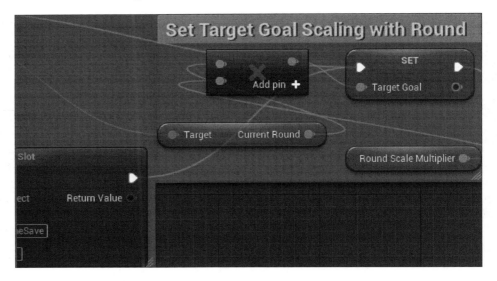

Begin by creating a new variable in the **My Blueprints** panel, and rename it to `RoundScaleMultiplier`. Change its **Variable Type** to **Integer**, and set the default value to a low number, such as 2. With a multiplier of 2, each round will add two more enemies that need to be defeated before the player can progress to the next round.

Now that we have a multiplier variable, we will multiply it with the current round information stored in the save file, and use the result for `TargetGoal`. First, drag a wire from the **Save Game to Slot** node's output execution pin, and attach it to a **Set Target Goal** node. Also, connect the output execution pin of the **Set Save Game Instance** node that ends the loading sequence to the same **Set Target Goal** node so that both the save object creation and save object loading branches end on the same node.

Next, drag a wire from one of the **Set Save Game Instance** nodes' output pins, and attach it to a **Get Current Round** node. Attach the output pin of this node to an **Integer * Integer** node. Then drag the `RoundScaleMultipler` variable onto the bottom input pin of the newly created **Integer * Integer** node. Finally, attach the output pin of this node to the input **Target Goal** pin of **Set Target Goal**. Even though these nodes are connected to our save creation and loading logic, scaling the target goal is a relatively independent function that happens to trigger off the same event. As such, select all four nodes that you just created and give them their own comment box in order to leave you with a reminder of their purpose.

The final step for establishing our game initialization logic is to reconnect the HUD creation and drawing nodes, along with the connected stamina recharge timer, to the sequence we have just concluded. Connect the output execution pin of the **Set Target Goal** node to the **Create HUD_C Widget** node's input execution node, as seen in this screenshot:

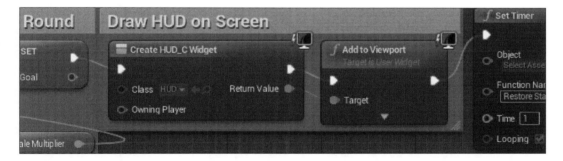

Create a transition screen to be shown between rounds

Currently, when the player defeats enough enemies to meet the requirements displayed by `TargetGoal`, they are presented with a win menu. It congratulates them and offers the opportunity to restart the game or quit out of the application. Now that we are adopting a round-based gameplay, we want to replace this win menu with a transition screen that will bring the player into the next round of gameplay.

We will start by making substantial modifications to our `WinMenu` Blueprint widget. Go to the **Content Browser** and open the **UI** folder. Rename the **WinMenu** Blueprint to `RoundTransition` so that it more accurately reflects its new purpose. Now open the **RoundTransition** Blueprint.

First, go to the **Hierarchy** panel and select the **Quit Button** object. Delete this button, as we will not need to present an option to quit during the round transitions. Next, click on the **Restart Button** object, and rename it to `Begin Round Button`. Click on the **Text** object nested underneath the button object, and in the **Details** panel, and change the text from `You Win!` to `Begin Round`. Finally, move this button to the lower-middle part of the canvas.

After that, select and delete the **You Win!** text block object. From the **Palette** panel, search for and drag down a new **Horizontal Box** object. Name this box `Round Display`. Back in the **Palette** panel, search for a **Text** object, and drag two of them down to the **Hierarchy** panel, placing them both on top of the **Round Display** object we created.

Select the first of these **Text** objects, and look at the **Details** panel. Change the **Text** field to `Round`, including the space. Also change the font size to be `150`. Now select the other `Text` object. Change its font size to `150` as well, and change its **Text** field to any two-digit number. Finally, select the parent **Round Display** object again, and resize the box until both the round text and the two-digit number can be seen fully. Place this object above the **Begin Round** button on the canvas. The final result of this layout should resemble the following screenshot:

Now we need to add behavior to this screen. Because the **Begin Round** button is merely a renamed version of the old **Restart** button, and we want the functionality of reloading the level to remain the same, we can leave this button alone. The additional binding behavior we need is to adjust the round number to match the round stored in the current save file. To start this process, click on the number text object, shown as **10** in the preceding screenshot, and then click on the **Bind** button next to the **Text** field in the **Details** panel. Next, click on the **Create Binding** option.

Our goal for this binding is to extract the current round from the saved game and show it on the screen in the form of text. The nodes used to accomplish this can be seen in the screenshot that follows:

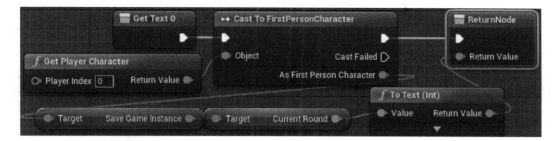

The current round is accessible through the save game instance variable attached to our player character, so we must first cast to that Blueprint to extract the save game information. Attach a **Cast to FirstPersonCharacter** node to the initial **Get Text 0** node, and then connect the output execution pin of that node to the **ReturnNode** that concludes this binding. Now drag the **Object** input pin of the casting node out, and attach it to a **Get Player Character** node.

With the player character referenced, we drag a wire from the **As First Person Character** output pin, and attach it to a **Get Save Game Instance** node. Then attach the output pin of this node to a **Get Current Round** node. With this information in hand, we can convert the data to text. Attach the output pin of the **Get Current Round** node to the **Return Value** input pin of **ReturnNode**, and a **To Text (Int)** translation node will be created for you automatically. Compile and save the **RoundTransition** Blueprint to finish your work here.

Transitioning to a new round when the current round is won

Now that we have a transition screen to display, we want to integrate it into our end game sequence, and combine it with the nodes that will increment the round each time the player beats their target goal. Return to the **FirstPersonCharacter** Blueprint, located inside the **Blueprints** folder of the **Content Browser**, to start working toward this goal.

Find the sequence of nodes you modified to branch between the win and lose menus that are triggered by the **End Game** event. From the **Branch** node, delete the **Create WinMenu_C Widget** and **Add to Viewport** nodes that are attached to the **False** output execution pin. We will be replacing these with nodes that increase the round by one and save that new round number in the save file, before displaying the transition screen. The Blueprint nodes meant for calculating and saving the current round number can be seen in the following screenshot:

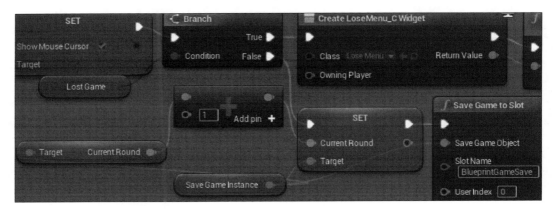

Begin by dragging and dropping the **SaveGameInstance** variable onto the grid below the **Branch** node, and then selecting the **Get** option from the menu that appears. Then drag a wire out from this node and attach it to a **Set Current Round** node. Attach the input execution pin of this node to the **False** output execution pin of the **Branch** node. Next, we need to calculate the integer that will be set as the current round.

Drag a second wire from the **Get Save Game Instance** node and attach it to a **Get Current Round** node. Now attach this node to an **Integer + Integer** node. Fill in the bottom input field with the number 1, and then attach the output pin of this node to the **Current Round** input pin of **Set Current Round** node. Finally, store this information in the save file by dragging a third wire from the **Get Save Game Instance** node and attaching it to a **Save Game to Slot** node. Attach the input and output execution pins of this node and the **Set Current Round** node, and then fill in the **Slot Name** input field with BlueprintGameSave.

Next, we need to call the round transition screen we created and draw it on the viewport, as seen in this screenshot:

Attach a **Create Widget** node to the **Save Game to Slot** node, and select **Round Transition** from the **Class** input drop-down menu. Then drag a wire from the **Return Value** output pin of this node and attach it to an **Add to Viewport** node. Finalize this sequence by ensuring that the execution pins of the **Create Widget** and **Add to Viewport** nodes are connected. We are now ready to test whether our round system is functional. Compile and save this Blueprint, and click on the **Play** button to test.

When you load the game, you should notice that the target goal counter at the top of the game has a low number of enemies as the goal. Defeat the number of enemies indicated by the goal and you should see the round transition screen appear, displaying **Round 2**. When you press the **Begin Round** button, you will be reloading the level, with your health and ammo restored, but with a higher number of enemies as the target. Defeat the number of enemies shown by the new target, and then you should be presented with the **Round 3** transition screen. Finally, if you quit the game and then click on the **Play** button again, you should find that the game loads the round that you were last on.

Pausing the game and resetting the save file

Now that we have the ability to track the player's progress, we should offer them the ability to reset their save file if they wish to begin the game from the start. We can accomplish this through the addition of a *pause* menu, which has the added benefit of allowing the player to take a temporary break in the action.

Creating a pause menu

First, we will create a pause menu that will present the player with options to resume playing the game, reset the game to round one, or to quit the application. Begin by going to the **UI** folder in the **Content Browser**. Right-click on **LoseMenu** and select the **Duplicate** option. Rename this new Blueprint widget to PauseMenu and open it.

Select the text displaying **You Lose. Try Again?**, and in the **Details** panel, change the **Text** field to say Paused.... Change the text color to a color you feel is appropriate for a pause message. Now select the **Restart** button's text object, and change the **Text** field to Resume.

Next, we will add a third button to allow the player to reset the save file. From the **Palette** panel, drag down a **Button** object into **Hierarchy**, dropping it onto the **CanvasPanel** object. Rename the button object to Reset Button. Then drag a **Text** object down from **Palette** and drop it onto **Reset Button**.

Select the text object on **Reset Button**, and change the **Text** field to Reset All. Also change the font size to 60, change the font color to black, and set **Justification** to center alignment. Now click on the **Reset Button** object, and in the **Details** panel, change the **Size X** field to 400.0 and the **Size Y** field to 150.0. Next, select the other two buttons and change their *x* and *y* sizes to the same values.

Now arrange all the three buttons along the center of the canvas, inserting the **Reset All** button between the **Resume** and **Quit** buttons. The final layout should resemble the following screenshot:

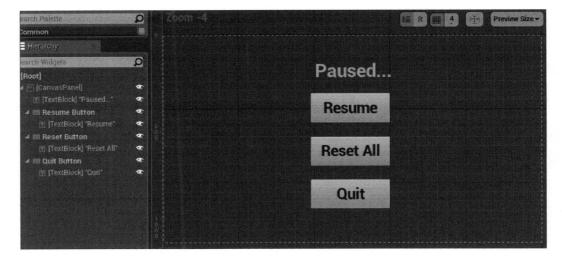

Resuming and resetting the save file

The next step is to modify the functionality of the pause screen buttons so that they can properly resume the game or reset the save file on the player's machine. Click on the **Reset All** button, and in the **Details** panel, click on the **+** button next to **OnClicked** to create a new button event. We will start by setting up the series of nodes needed to resume the game from a paused state, as seen in this screenshot:

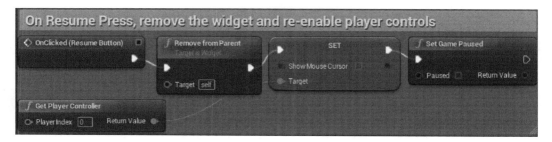

In the **Graph** view, delete the **Open Level** node attached to the resume button event, and then connect the **Remove from Parent** node directly to the **OnClicked (Resume Button)** node. In addition to removing the pause menu when **Resume** is clicked on, we need to resume the game and disable the mouse arrow.

Create a new **Get Player Controller** node. Drag a wire from the **Return Value** output pin of this node and attach it to a **Set Show Mouse Cursor** node. Ensure that this node's **Show Mouse Cursor** input checkbox is unchecked, and attach the input execution pin of this node to the output execution pin of the **Remove from Parent** node. Finally, attach the output execution pin of the **Set Show Mouse Cursor** node to a **Set Game Paused** node, while ensuring that the **Paused** input checkbox is left unchecked. That will complete the functionality of the **Resume** button.

Now turn your attention to the **OnClicked (Reset Button)** node. We will first be checking for the existence of a save game to be reset, and if one is found, we will use the player character to set the new save data. The nodes needed to handle the save game branch and player character casting can be seen here:

Drag a wire from the output execution pin of the **OnClicked (Reset Button)** node, and attach it to a **Does Save Game Exist** node. In the **Slot Name** input of this node, type `BlueprintGameSave`, ensuring that your spelling is consistent with the slot names given in the core logic within **FirstPersonCharacter**.

Next, drag a wire from the **Return Value** output pin and attach it to a **Branch** node. Attach the **True** output execution pin of the **Branch** node to a **Cast To FirstPersonCharacter** node. Finally, drag a wire from the **Object** input pin of the casting node and attach it to the **Get Player Character** node.

Now that we have the player character, we need to grab its save game instance and reset the current round to the first round. We will then need to save this updated save game information to the **BlueprintGameSave** slot on the player's machine.

Stat by dragging a wire from the **As First Person Character** output pin of the **Cast To FirstPersonCharacter** node and attaching it to a **Get Save Game Instance** node. Next, drag a wire from the output pin of this node to the **Set Current Round** node. Ensure that the execution pins between this node and the **Cast To FirstPersonCharacter** node are connected, and set the input **Current Round** field to 1. Because the only data we intend to persist across play sessions is the current round the player is on, this is the only information we need to overwrite to represent a fresh save game.

Now we need to ensure that our updated round data is actually stored in the player's machine. Drag a second wire from the output pin of the **Get Save Game Instance** node, and attach it to a **Save Game to Slot** node. Connect the input execution pin of this node to the output execution pin of the **Set Current Round** node, and write `BlueprintGameSave` for the **Slot Name** input field. The results of this should look like what is shown in the following screenshot:

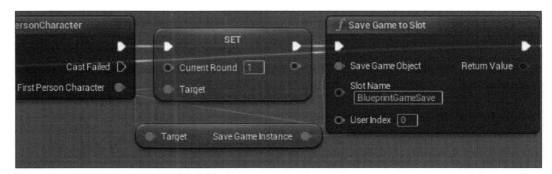

The final step for our **Reset** button is to reload the game map and remove the pause menu at the end of the sequence, as shown in this screenshot:

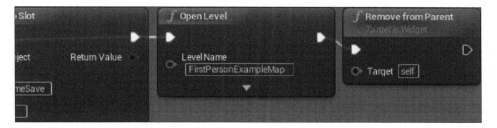

Drag a wire from the output execution pin from the **Save Game to Slot** node to an **Open Level** node. Then look all the way back to the **Branch** node described earlier, drag a wire from the **False** output execution pin of that node, and connect it to the **Open Level** node. This will ensure that even if there is no save game data to overwrite, the button will still give some feedback by starting the game with the first round. For the **LevelName** input field of the **Open Level** node, enter either **FirstPersonExampleMap** or the name of your level, if you have chosen to rename it differently from our example. Finally, connect a wire from the output execution pin of the **Open Level** node to a new **Remove from Parent** node. Congratulations! That concludes our work on the pause menu functionality. Create a helpful comment for the reset button nodes, and then compile and save the Blueprint to finish.

Triggering the pause menu

Now that we have created our pause menu, we need a way for the player to bring up the menu. Traditionally, computer games use the *Esc* key to pause the game and return to a menu, so we will follow that trope here. First, we will bind the *Esc* key to a pause action. Just as we did back in *Chapter 2*, *Enhancing Player Abilities*, we will be adding a new action mapping inside **Project Settings**. On the **Edit** button in the Unreal Editor menu, select the **Project Settings** option. On the left side of the window that appears, look for the **Engine** category and select the **Input** option. Click on the **+** sign next to **Action Mappings**, and call the mapping `Pause`. Use the drop-down menu to select the **Escape Key** mapping.

Like all other actions the player can take, we want to establish the functionality of this action within the **FirstPersonCharacter** Blueprint. Go to the **Content Browser** and open the **FirstPersonCharacter** Blueprint inside the **Blueprints** folder. You can see the nodes we will be building to bring up the pause menu in the following screenshot:

First, find some empty grid space and add an **InputAction Pause** event node. Since bringing up the pause menu will disrupt the gameplay, it will feel better if the action is taken only when the user releases the *Esc* key, as opposed to when they first press it. Drag a wire from the **Released** output pin of the **Escape** node, and attach it to a **Set Game Paused** node. Ensure that the **Paused** input checkbox of this node is checked.

With the game paused, we need to enable the mouse arrow so that the player can click on the menu buttons. Start by creating a **Get Player Controller** node, and drag a wire from its **Return Value** output pin to a **Set Show Mouse Cursor** node. Check the **Show Mouse Cursor** input box to set the mouse arrow to appear on the screen. Afterwards, connect the input execution pin of this node to the output execution pin of the **Set Game Paused** node.

With the game paused and the cursor enabled, we can bring up the **Pause Menu** UI we created. Drag a wire from the output execution pin of the **Set Show Mouse Cursor** node and attach it to a **Create Widget** node. Select **Pause Menu** from the **Class** input drop-down menu. Then, drag a wire from the **Return Value** output pin of this node and attach it to an **Add to Viewport** node. Connect the execution pins between these two nodes to finish this series of nodes. Remember to add a helpful comment container around the nodes, and then compile and save this Blueprint.

We will have to make a slight alteration to our testing strategy to test the pause menu. The *Esc* key, by default, closes any active windows currently playing the game within the editor. Thus, the game would close before we could see the pause menu we created. There are two ways by which we can get around this. We can change the key to bring up the pause menu to something other than *Esc*, such as the *P* key. Alternatively, we can change the **Play** mode in the editor to generate a standalone game window. To follow the latter option, click on the downward-facing arrow next to the **Play** button, and select the **Standalone Game** option, as seen in the following screenshot:

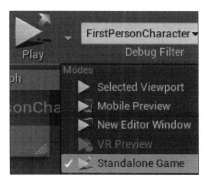

Now, while playing, you should be able to press the *Esc* key you set up to bring up the pause menu. Clicking on the **Resume** button should close the pause menu and return you to the game. If you progress several rounds through the game and then press the **Reset All** button from the pause menu, you should automatically reload the level, with your progress reset to the first round of the game. If this is what you see, then congratulations! You have accomplished a significant achievement in creating a save system that is able to store, load, and reset progress across multiple rounds of gameplay.

Summary

In this chapter, we made significant strides toward making our game a complete experience that can be played and enjoyed by other people. You learned how to branch the end states of the game based on whether the player has won or lost. You also learned to implement a *save system* that allows the player to return to their earlier game sessions, with their progress intact. Then, we implemented a round system that modifies the gameplay goal each time the player progresses to a new round. Finally, we implemented additional menu systems that give the player information about which round they are on, and give them the opportunity to pause the gameplay and even reset their own save file.

This represents the entire game experience we will be creating in the book. In the next chapter, we will explore making and publishing builds of the game we created so that we can share the experience with others. In addition, we will look back at how far your skills have developed, and then look forward and discuss how you can pursue further learning and extend this game to be even better.

8
Building and Publishing

One of the best ways to grow as a game developer is to share your work with others so that you can get feedback on how to evolve your designs and content. An early priority should be to create sharable builds of your game so that other people can play the experience for themselves. Fortunately, Unreal Engine 4 makes it extremely simple to create builds of your game that can work across multiple platforms. In this final chapter, we will look at how to optimize the settings of our game, the process of building for your target desktop platform, and how you might approach developing for mobile devices, game consoles, or web browsers. In the process, we will cover the following topics:

- Optimizing graphics settings
- Creating a packaged game to share with others
- Identifying resources for further learning and development

Optimizing your graphics settings

Prior to creating a **build**, or a version of our game that has been optimized to play on a particular platform, you should change the graphics settings of our game to ensure that they are suited for your target machines. The graphics settings in Unreal Engine 4 are identified as **Engine Scalability Settings**. This setting interface is composed of several graphics settings, each of which determines the final visual quality of one element of the game. With any game, there is a trade-off between high-quality effects and visuals, and the performance of that game in terms of frame rate.

Games that struggle with a low frame rate performance feel bad from a gameplay perspective, even if the mechanics are otherwise solid. As such, it is important to balance the desire to make your game look as good as it can with the need to understand what the performance impact will be on the machines that your players will be running the game on. Because of the varying hardware performance of PCs and Mac computers, many games targeting those platforms use custom menu settings to allow the player to tweak the graphics settings of the game themselves. However, the game we have created only uses very simple assets and a relatively constrained level size, so we are going to simply define some workable defaults before generating a build to distribute.

To access **Engine Scalability Settings**, go to the **FirstPersonExampleMap** tab and look at the level editor toolbar at the top. Click on the **Settings** button, and hover over **Engine Scalability Settings** to see a pop out display of the **Quality** settings you can tweak, as seen in the following screenshot:

The buttons along the top of this menu, ranging from **Low** to **Epic,** serve as presets of the settings based on the broad level of performance versus quality that you want to target. Clicking on the **Low** button will set all the quality settings to the minimum, giving you the best possible performance, in exchange for the least visually attractive settings. **Epic** is the opposite end of the spectrum, raising all of the engine quality settings to their maximum, at the sacrifice of significant performance, depending on the assets you have chosen to use.

The **Auto** button will detect the hardware of the machine you are currently running the editor on, and adjust the graphics settings to a level that strikes a good balance between performance and quality of graphics for your machine. If you are intending to target hardware that is roughly equivalent to the machine you are developing on, using the **Auto** setting can be a simple way to establish the graphics settings for your build. If you wish to tweak these settings individually, you can use this brief description of their functions:

- **Resolution Scale**: This setting causes the engine to render the game in a lower resolution than the resolution that your player will be targeting, and uses software to upscale the game to the targeted resolution. This improves the performance of the game, at the cost of perceived fuzziness at lower resolution scales.

- **View Distance**: This determines how far from the camera location objects are rendered. Shorter view distances increase performance, but can cause objects to pop into view.

- **Anti-Aliasing**: This setting softens the jagged edges of 3D objects in the world, which can dramatically improve the looks of your game. However, this filter comes at a significant performance cost.

- **Post-Processing**: This setting changes the baseline quality settings of several filters that get applied to the screen after the scene is created, such as motion blur or light bloom effects.

- **Shadows**: This changes the baseline quality of several bundled settings that combine to determine the look of shadows in the game. Highly detailed shadows often have a dramatic impact on performance.

- **Textures**: This setting will affect the process by which the textures used in your game are managed by the engine. If you have many large textures in your game, reducing this setting can help avoid running out of graphics memory, and thus increase performance.

- **Effects**: This setting changes the baseline quality settings of several special effects applied to the game, such as material reflections or translucency effects.

Ultimately, the best way of optimizing the performance of your game is to regularly test it on the machines you intend for people to play it on. If you notice sluggish performance, take note of where you see it occur. If the performance of your game is always low, you might need to reduce some of the post-processing or anti-aliasing effects. If performance is low only in certain areas of your level, you might need to look at reducing the object density in that area, or reduce the quality of a particular game model.

Setting up our game to be played by others

Unreal Engine 4 offers a wide variety of platforms that you can choose from to build your game, and this list will continue to expand as newer versions of the engine are released and new technologies emerge. Currently, you can deploy your game on Windows PC, Mac OS X, iOS, Android, Linux, SteamOS, and HTML 5. This engine also supports creation of content that utilizes the various emerging virtual reality platforms, such as **Oculus Rift**. If you are a registered console developer with the appropriate development kit, you will be pleased to know that Unreal Engine 4 also supports creating games for the Xbox One and PlayStation 4. Each platform has its own unique requirements and best practices associated with it. Mobile games and web (HTML5) games in particular have higher optimization requirements in order to get games to perform well on those platforms.

Creating a distributable form of your game for one of these platforms involves a process called **packaging**. Packaging takes all of the code and assets of the game and sets them up in the proper format to perform on the selected platform. We will be following the path to making a Windows PC or Max OS X release of your game.

It is important to note that Unreal Engine 4 can only create Windows builds from a copy of the engine running on a Windows PC, and OS X builds from copies installed on a Mac running OS X. Thus, the platforms that you can target with your game will be partially limited by the machine you are developing the game on. If you are developing on a Windows PC and wish to create an OS X build of the game, you can install another copy of Unreal Engine 4 on a Mac, and copy your project files to this new machine. From there, you will be able to generate an OS X build, with no further changes required.

First, we may want to customize some of the settings that will determine how our project appears on the target machine. To do so, click on the **Settings** button in the level editor toolbar, and then click on **Project Settings**, as shown here:

Inside **Project Settings**, you will see a wide variety of options in the left panel for customization of different aspects of the game, engine, and platform interactions. By default, the **Project – Description** page will open. Here, you can customize the project name, the icon as it will appear in the Unreal Engine project selector, and a brief description of the project and its creator or publisher, as shown in this screenshot:

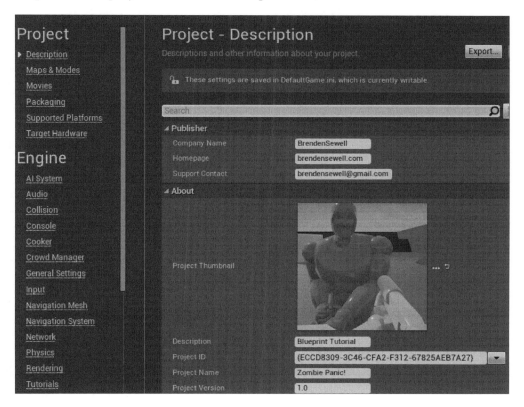

Clicking on **Maps & Modes** will bring you to a page where you can determine which map the game will load by default. Our game has only one map, so that makes this choice easy, but often you will need to designate a map dedicated to your main menu screen to be the first map to load. When you create games with multiple maps, you will need to ensure that the first map loaded is able to manage which map is loaded next in the play experience. This is similar to how we determined which round to activate when we loaded our game from an existing save file:

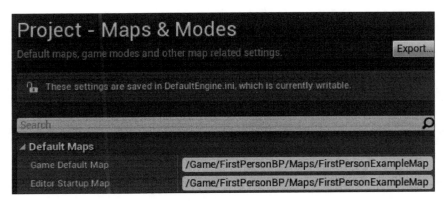

Finally, clicking on the platform you are targeting with the build will bring you to that platform's customization page. In the **Mac** example shown in the following screenshot, only the **Splash** screens and the game **Icon** image are available for changing. Mobile and console platform targets will have more options to change, which will be specific to each of those platforms:

Replace the default **Splash** and **Icon** settings with the images you would like to use for your game. This can be as simple as an edited screenshot from the game, or you can show off a custom piece of art made specifically for icons and splash screens. Once you are satisfied with your project settings, leave the **Project Settings** window.

Packaging the game into a build

To package your game to be played on a particular platform, click on **File** in the main menu, then on **Package Project**, and finally on the relevant platform that matches the build you want to make, like this:

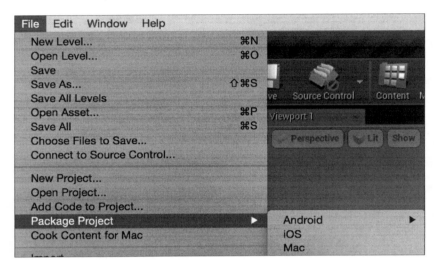

Once you click on a platform, you will be prompted to select a location on your hard drive to store the build you make. After selecting a location, you will see a popup that tells you that the engine is packaging the project. If something goes wrong in the packaging process, you will be shown the details of the error in the output log window that pops up. Packaging a project can take a bit of time, depending on how complex and large the project is, but if you don't encounter any errors, then you will eventually see a message saying that the packaging is complete. Congratulations, you have created a completed copy of your game!

Navigate to the folder where you chose to store your build. On a Mac, open the folder called MacNoEditor and double-click on the application to launch it. For Windows, open the WindowsNoEditor folder and double-click on the executable to run the game. Take a moment to go through the game you created in its final form, and reflect on just how far you have come. You now have a functional game that you can have other people play and enjoy. Making even simple games is no easy feat, so you should feel proud of your accomplishment!

Steps for further learning

As you look ahead past the experiences and skills gained from following this book, you should formulate strategies to enhance your development skills further. If you follow the upcoming advice, you will not only enhance your skills as a developer, but also be able to share your knowledge with the wider Unreal Engine development community, helping other new learners in the process.

Finish and share as many games as you can

Whether you are looking to start a career with a studio in the commercial gaming industry or you want to become a successful independent game developer, the most important advice for honing your skills to succeed is to develop and release as many games as you can. Game development is both an art and a science. The best way to gain the insights and confidence you need to evolve into a great developer is by releasing games and receiving feedback that will push you to grow.

The skills you learned in this book focused on giving you the scripting knowledge necessary to be able to create a fully functional game. However, there is no reason to stop here! Take your time to explore the game you have developed, and add more levels, mechanics, and art. Post your project online to start getting feedback from friends and members of the Unreal development community. Try experimental gameplay features and rapidly prototype them for feedback, or polish your games until they become something you can release to a wider audience and showcase as the best that you can accomplish. The important thing is to finish and release your game. After that, start another project! Create a website portfolio that contains playable forms of the games you have created, and tells a bit about the process you went through to make them. If you decide to start charging money for your games, you can add a storefront to your portfolio, from which you can advertise and allow people to purchase your games.

If you are applying for a job at a studio, the most important thing you can do to give them confidence in your abilities is show them that you have the skills and discipline required to take a game from a concept to a shipped project. As an independent game developer, releasing multiple games early will allow you to gain valuable feedback from your audience so that you know what is working and what is not. It will also begin the process of forming a community around your game releases, generating excitement for each new game that you create.

Stretch out of your comfort zone

The domain of game development involves numerous skills and disciplines coming together to develop interactive experiences. Although many of the best game developers bring with them years of in-depth experience in a particular domain, such as character modeling or AI programming, all developers benefit from some level of knowledge that cuts across disciplines. As you continue to develop your own skills using Unreal Engine 4 as your tool set, it is important to push yourself continually to expand your knowledge into aspects of game development that you are not yet comfortable with. Although this book focused on the game mechanics and functionality you can build using visual scripting, expanding your skill set into modeling, animation, and design will make you a more versatile developer and increase the quality of the games that you independently develop.

Resources for additional learning and support

There are many resources available for you to continue broadening your skills. As you pursue Unreal Engine development, I recommend that you regularly reference the official documentation (`https://docs.unrealengine.com/latest/INT/`) to see the latest instructions on the feature sets of the engine. When you are attempting to approach a new feature for the first time or need to figure out what a specific option does to a feature about which you have already been learning, the official documentation should be the first place you look.

The Unreal Engine answers page (`https://answers.unrealengine.com/`) allows you to browse questions and answers provided by other Unreal developers. For most development challenges that you will face when making games, you will find another developer who has faced the same issue. If you are struggling on a particularly difficult problem and the documentation isn't leading you to an answer, the Unreal Engine answers page should be one of the first places you look at, to see whether someone else has already overcome this challenge. If nobody has yet asked the question for which you are seeking help, you should post it yourself so that the entire community can benefit from your learning process. Sometimes, you will receive suggestions about a different way of tackling the problem you posted that makes it less complex and more manageable.

The Unreal Engine community forums (`https://forums.unrealengine.com/`) will also be available for you, and should be referenced for helpful advice from other developers using the tool set. You can ask discipline-specific questions on the forms, see other people's working projects and code samples, or post status updates on your work in progress and get feedback on your games from the broader community.

When you set out to ask a question using any of the preceding resources, first remember to search and check whether the question has already been answered before. Most of the time, you will find that it already has. In this way, you can ensure that when you do ask a question, you are contributing something useful to the community. Make sure you include in your question detailed information about what you are trying to accomplish and what you have already tried. This will maximize the chances of someone else being able to provide the information that will allow you to succeed.

Summary

In this chapter, we discussed creating playable builds of the game we created across multiple platforms. We also discussed how you could begin getting feedback about your game from users, and where you can access additional resources to learn more about game development with Unreal Engine 4.

From me and everyone involved in the creation of this book, thank you for reading! I hope you have enjoyed following the examples and learning about visual scripting. Remember that this is just the beginning of your journey toward creating the games you want to develop. I wish you best of luck on all of your future endeavors in game development.

Index

A

actor 5
AI Controller 87
ammo
  counter, reducing 59
  tracking 59
anchors 51

B

Behavior Tree
  about 86
  conditions, adding 97, 98
  hearing, adding 107
  wandering, adding 126, 127
binding
  creating 55
Blackboard 87
Blueprints
  character movement, breaking down 30-32
  control inputs, customizing 32
  creating 10, 11
  Event Graph panel, exploring 12, 13
  extending, for adding running
      functionality 30
  hit detection event, creating 13
  improving 16-18
  material, swapping 14, 15
  sprint ability, adding 33-35
build
  about 151
  game, packaging into 158

C

canvas 50
chasing behavior
  creating 99-101
collectable objects
  creating 71
collection logic
  setting up 72-75
compiling process 15
custom event 65

D

decorator node 98
delta time
  used, for obtaining relative speed 22
direction
  changing 25
  moving targets, testing 26

E

eliminated targets
  counter, increasing 60
  tracking 59
emitter 44
enemy
  Blueprint content, reusing 116-118
  chasing behavior, creating 99-101
  conditions, adding to Behavior Tree 97, 98
  hearing, adding to Behavior Tree 107
  investigating tasks, seeding 108-110
  making, destructible 115

creating 88
patrol points, setting up 88
NavMesh
used, for making level traversable 85, 86
node 7
noise event data
interpreting 111-113
storing 111-113
normalizing 22

O

objects
adding, to level 5
Oculus Rift 154

P

packaging 154
pause menu
creating 144
triggering 147-149
Pawn Sensing
used, for granting enemy sight 95-97
player
chasing, with AI 95
player actions, constraining
about 64
actions, blocking with branch 69
firing actions, preventing 71
looping timers, used for repeating
actions 67-69
stamina, draining while sprinting 64-66
stamina, regenerating 70, 71
project
creating 1-4
first level, creating 1, 2
settings, adjusting 4
template, setting 3

R

round-based scaling
creating, with saved games 133
enemy target goal, increasing 138, 139
game information, storing with
SaveGame object 133, 134

new round, transitioning to 141-143
saved data, loading 134-138
saved data, storing 134-138
transition screen, creating 139-141
running functionality
adding, by extending Blueprint 30

S

save file
resetting 143-147
resuming 145-147
Selector 93
Sequence 93
sound and particle effects
adding 40
destruction, triggering 43-45
explosions, triggering 43-45
sound effects, triggering 43-45
targets state, checking with branch
node 40-42
spawn limits
managing, with variables 119, 120
spawn point
of enemy appearance, selecting 118
spawn rates
managing, with variables 119, 120
static 19

T

target point 88
task nodes 93
timeline 36
transform 23

U

UI meters
ammo, creating 52, 53
appearance, customizing 50, 51
creating, with UMG 47, 48
enemy counters, creating 52, 53
HUD, displaying 54, 55
shapes, drawing with widget
Blueprints 48-50

UI values
  bindings for health, creating 55, 56
  bindings for stamina, creating 55, 56
  connecting, to player variables 55
  text bindings, creating 57, 58
Unreal Engine 4
  URL 1
**Unreal Motion Graphics UI Designer
    (UMG)**
  used, for creating simple UI 48
  used, for creating simple UI meters 47

V

vector 21
viewport 5

W

widget Blueprints
  used, for drawing shapes 48-50
wire 8

Z

zoom view
  animating 36
  projectile's speed, increasing 39, 40
  timeline, used for transition
      smoothing 36-39

Thank you for buying
Blueprints Visual Scripting for Unreal Engine

About Packt Publishing

Packt, pronounced 'packed', published its first book, *Mastering phpMyAdmin for Effective MySQL Management*, in April 2004, and subsequently continued to specialize in publishing highly focused books on specific technologies and solutions.

Our books and publications share the experiences of your fellow IT professionals in adapting and customizing today's systems, applications, and frameworks. Our solution-based books give you the knowledge and power to customize the software and technologies you're using to get the job done. Packt books are more specific and less general than the IT books you have seen in the past. Our unique business model allows us to bring you more focused information, giving you more of what you need to know, and less of what you don't.

Packt is a modern yet unique publishing company that focuses on producing quality, cutting-edge books for communities of developers, administrators, and newbies alike. For more information, please visit our website at www.packtpub.com.

Writing for Packt

We welcome all inquiries from people who are interested in authoring. Book proposals should be sent to author@packtpub.com. If your book idea is still at an early stage and you would like to discuss it first before writing a formal book proposal, then please contact us; one of our commissioning editors will get in touch with you.

We're not just looking for published authors; if you have strong technical skills but no writing experience, our experienced editors can help you develop a writing career, or simply get some additional reward for your expertise.

**UnrealScript Game
Programming Cookbook**

ISBN: 978-1-84969-556-5   Paperback: 272 pages

Discover how you can augment your game
development with the power of UnrealScript

1. Create a truly unique experience within UDK
   using a series of powerful recipes to augment
   your content.

2. Discover how you can utilize the advanced
   functionality offered by the Unreal Engine
   with UnrealScript.

3. Learn how to harness the built-in AI in UDK
   to its full potential.

**Learning Unreal® Engine iOS
Game Development**

ISBN: 978-1-78439-771-5   Paperback: 212 pages

Create exciting iOS games with the power
of the new Unreal® Engine 4 subsystems

1. Learn about the entire iOS pipeline, from
   game creation to game submission.

2. Develop exciting iOS games with the Unreal
   Engine 4.x toolset.

3. Step-by-step tutorials to build optimized
   iOS games.

Please check **www.PacktPub.com** for information on our titles

Unreal Development Kit Game Design Cookbook

ISBN: 978-1-84969-180-2   Paperback: 544 pages

Over 100 recipes to accelerate the process of learning game design with UDKk

1. An intermediate, fast-paced UDK guide for game artists.

2. The quickest way to face the challenges of game design with UDK.

3. All the necessary steps to get your artwork up and running in game.

4. Part of Packt's Cookbook series: Each recipe is a carefully organized sequence of instructions to complete the task as efficiently as possible.

Unreal Development Kit Beginner's Guide

ISBN: 978-1-84969-052-2   Paperback: 244 pages

A fun, quick, step-by-step guide to level design and creating your own game world

1. Full of illustrations, diagrams, and tips for creating your first level and game environment.

2. Clear step-by-step instructions and fun practical examples.

3. Master the essentials of level design and environment creation.

Please check **www.PacktPub.com** for information on our titles

Made in the USA
Middletown, DE
26 October 2015